# the
# Blues
# are up

## CARDIFF CITY'S

### RISE TO THE PREMIER LEAGUE

*For Anna, Ava and Noah*

# the Blues are up

## CARDIFF CITY'S

### RISE TO THE PREMIER LEAGUE

## Scott Johnson

First impression: 2013
© Scott Johnson & Y Lolfa Cyf., 2013

The publishers wish to acknowledge the support of
Cyngor Llyfrau Cymru

Cover photograph: Mike Vaughan
Cover design: Y Lolfa

ISBN:  978 184771 739 9

Printed on acid-free and partly recycled paper
and published and bound in Wales by
Y Lolfa Cyf., Talybont, Ceredigion SY24 5HE
*e-mail* ylolfa@ylolfa.com
*website* www.ylolfa.com
*tel* 01970 832 304
*fax* 832 782

# Forewords

'The 2012–13 season is the year that fans of Cardiff City will talk about in the city's pubs and valley drinking holes for years and years to come. No more near-misses, tales of hard luck or players sold during the season to deny the Bluebirds promotion – no, it will be about Craig Bellamy's infectious will to win, Mark Hudson and David Marshall's heroics at the back, Peter Whittingham's delivery and the Malky Mackay victory punch. This is the year promotion to the top flight was delivered. The dream became reality and the Cardiff City Stadium started making its own history and a place in the fans' hearts. This is your reward for all the support and miles covered in your own personal journeys following the City. Enjoy the Premier League and continue to sing your hearts out for the boys!'

**Jason Perry**

(Jason Perry spent 11 seasons at Cardiff City, making 333 appearances between 1986–97, captained the side with distinction and also represented Wales at international level)

'Cardiff has been a huge part of my career and my life, my son was born there and the club gave me a platform to play. Sam Hammam gave me the challenge of helping the club get promoted, which we managed in my second season. The play-off final very much felt like a home game for us in Cardiff, we had that pressure on us and we had to perform. I can't imagine what it would have felt like had we lost that day, it instead gave the whole city a lift. Malky has done a fantastic job at the football club in his two years in charge. He's a very steady manager, very level-headed. His teams are very well organised but they play with flair. It's important that Cardiff sign the right calibre of player, as the squad they have at the moment is inexperienced. It's all about getting those 40 points in the Premier League and even if you finish one place above the drop zone, it will be a success.'

**Graham Kavanagh**

(Graham Kavanagh was Cardiff's first £1m signing in 2001, captained the side and represented the Republic of Ireland on 16 occasions)

'Having played for Swansea, it was tough at the beginning and I received some grief but I loved it at Cardiff. I had five years there in which we were always playing for something at the end of the year. We had some good managers and some good players and I always looked forward to playing in front of the Ninian Park faithful.

The Cardiff supporters deserve to be in the Premier League. The rebrand hurt a lot of fans but they stuck with their team, that tells you how good they are. They were brilliant to me when I had my illness, their support was incredible I owe them a big thank you.'

**Andy Legg**

(Andy Legg played 175 times for Cardiff and also represented Wales at international level)

# The edge of glory

IT WAS APPARENT that the 2012/13 season was different pretty early on in the campaign. I contribute blogs to Wales Online and wrote one in December entitled: "Five reasons why Cardiff City look like champions." Everything seemed to be working in their favour and I was very comfortable making this proclamation. Four months later, with three games still to spare, the 51-year wait for top-flight football was finally over.

Considerable summer investment in the squad was significant, but the reasons I outlined were the impressive work ethic instilled in the side by strict disciplinarian Malky Mackay and the even distribution of goals. I also highlighted the apparent lack of competition, the Craig Bellamy factor and plenty of room for improvement.

The performance that reinforced my belief and prompted the piece was City's emphatic 4–1 win at Blackburn, which extended their lead at the top of the table to four points. Cardiff completely controlled the contest, against a side recently relegated from the top flight, looking a Premier League side in all but status. They subsequently maintained their position and even managed to double their lead by the season's end.

Having observed the Championship up close in the past ten years, there are certain attributes that all serious promotion contenders exhibit. Tenacity, durability and an innate confidence were all present and accounted for. It was a thrill to see Cardiff embody these qualities and set the pace for the majority of the season with remarkable consistency.

For some, the achievement was tarnished by the controversial pre-season rebrand, while others viewed the change from blue to red as a means to an end. I personally remain opposed to the changes, but continue to attend games. It was a difficult season both morally and emotionally, but I have compartmentalised my feelings and can appreciate the achievements of the team detached from the politics behind the scenes.

I feel the season warrants a thorough review because money does not guarantee success and they have managed to exceed all expectations under difficult circumstances, while shouldering the weight of past failures.

Cardiff have since been linked with dozens of players and have already smashed their transfer record with the £8.5m signing of Copenhagen striker Andreas Cornelius. They have been linked with eight-figure offers for various other targets but, at the time of writing, the club were finding it difficult to spend the £25m sum earmarked by owner Vincent Tan. Fortunately, an agreement was finally reached with Langston in July for a long-standing debt, an obstacle which has been preventing Tan from converting his loans into equity.

The new kit release caused consternation, an all-red ensemble with mismatching shorts, which were changed to black after fans were allowed to vote between four different combinations. But the club has managed to retain the services of Mackay, which is a real boost after he was heavily linked with the vacant Everton job.

The prospect of them pitting their wits against the very best teams in the land is both daunting and exciting.

This book begins with a 2011/12 play-off defeat at West Ham – and in a strange twist of fate the 2013/14 fixture list has paired the two sides against each other on the opening day, bringing the journey full circle. Cardiff also defeated The Hammers at Upton Park in

Mackay's first match in charge, the first game of the 2011/12 season.

Hopefully history will repeat itself this August.

# A pre-season rebrand

28th July – Forest Green Rovers (a)
31st July – Cheltenham Town (a)

CARDIFF CITY ARE well-accustomed to the Championship. It is an unrelenting division, with very few easy games. Relegation-threatened strugglers can conquer sides pushing for automatic promotion on any given day. Over the course of 46 games, character is forged or exposed, while two games a week, almost every week, undoubtedly take their toll. And that's without taking into account the relentless travelling to and from games, coupled with the scars of previous failures – of which Cardiff have had more than their fair share.

During a decade spent in the second tier, Cardiff fans have endured plenty of near-misses and disappointment. After progressing from Division Two, now regarded as League One, in 2003 they spent an initial few seasons acclimatising to their new surroundings. Emerging as credible contenders for promotion during the 2008/09 season, they lost three of their last four games and missed out on the play-offs by a solitary goal. In the following season, they progressed through the play-offs and were beaten 3–2 by Blackpool in the final. In 2010/11, Cardiff crashed out at the semi-final stage against Reading, a defeat which cost manager Dave Jones his job.

Jones took over the club in 2005 amid financial chaos, as players were sold en masse to keep the club afloat and escalating debt threatened to consume the club. He rebuilt the team and often over-achieved, including taking Cardiff to the FA Cup final in 2008, overseeing a narrow 1–0 defeat by Portsmouth. He enjoyed a prickly relationship with the local press which eroded to such an extent that he eventually stopped talking to them. His demeanour became increasingly dour until he was finally relieved of his duties in May 2011. A new broom was required.

Malky Mackay was a no-nonsense centre back who represented Queen's Park and Celtic before heading to England in September 1998. Despite relatively limited ability, he represented his country at the age of 32, becoming the oldest Scottish debutant for 37 years. He also featured in three consecutive Championship promotion campaigns, for Norwich in 2004, West Ham in 2005 and Watford in 2006. His tenacity and experience were surely qualities that appealed to the Cardiff board when they appointed him as manager in June 2011.

After fulfilling a bit-part role at Watford in the Premier League, Mackay became first-team coach in January 2007. He took charge for five games between the departure of Aidy Boothroyd in November 2008 and subsequent appointment of Brendan Rodgers, before inheriting the role on a permanent basis in June 2009, when Rodgers resigned. At the time, Watford chairman Jimmy Russo justified his decision by conceding: "Malky has all the attributes to be a good manager, he has great leadership skills and, crucially, gives us continuity at the club."

Mackay impressed during his season in charge at Vicarage Road, maximising the efforts of a small squad and supplementing them with shrewd loan signings. Watford eventually finished 14th and their best performance of the season was a 4–1 thrashing of Cardiff, which would prove to be instrumental in his relocation to South Wales.

When Alan Shearer turned down the Cardiff post, they turned to Mackay and agreed a compensation package with Watford. He inherited a first-team squad of only ten players, after twelve had departed before his arrival. Mackay moved swiftly to bring in Craig Conway, Don Cowie, Andrew Taylor, Robert Earnshaw,

Aron Gunnarsson, Joe Mason, Kenny Miller, Rudy Gestede and Ben Turner for just over £2m. He fashioned them in to a hard-working, high-intensity, cohesive whole that exceeded all expectations by making the play-offs. They also progressed to the final of the Carling Cup, losing on penalties to Liverpool. Competing on two fronts with a small squad resulted in West Ham comfortably beating Cardiff over two legs in the play-off semi-finals. A campaign rich in promise should have whetted the appetite of fans for what this group of players might achieve in future. Instead, their attention had been diverted towards a rumour that was spreading among fans that had made the trip to Upton Park. These claims culminated in an anonymous post by 'Blue Since 1908' on a Cardiff City message board later that evening:

*Apologies for the anonymous nature of this message, which will be my one and only post on this subject. Please be assured that the information contained herein is genuine and now this is out in the open, direct questions need to be asked of our club.*

*Now that the curtain has come down on Cardiff's season, there is some very important news that everyone needs to be made aware of. In recent weeks, deals have been agreed with Cardiff's largest creditors, which pave the way for the Malaysians to take full control of the club during the summer. Bankrolled by Vincent Tan, manager Malky Mackay will be provided with a war chest to take Cardiff to the Premier League, stadium expansion plans will go ahead and a multi-million pound training facility will be built. All this may sound like everything we have been waiting for, but there is one bitter pill to swallow. Cardiff City is about to be completely re-branded in a manner which goes against a century of our history.*

*Cardiff City will play in red next season. The dragon will become the major emblem on the club badge and the stadium will literally turn red. This change has been ordered by Vincent Tan and a red home kit and blue away kit have already been agreed for next season. The club intend to announce these changes over the next few days.*

*The investment into Cardiff City by the Malaysians over the last two years has been very welcome and almost certainly saved us from going into administration. It now seems that they are ready to take the next step and assume full control, but intend riding roughshod over our identity and changing our football club into something none of us will recognise or be able to identify with.*

*Cardiff City have played in blue since 1908. We*

*won the FA Cup and competed in the top flight in those colours, we are the Bluebirds. A huge part of our identity, history and tradition are bound up in the colours, badge and nickname of the club.*

*The Malaysians MUST NOT be allowed to proceed with these plans and destroy decades of history and tradition. There may be some fans that say so what, it doesn't matter what colour we play in as long as the club is progressing. Well if that is the case, just why do they want to change our identity? It smacks of a lack of knowledge of what a football club consists of and begs the question of what other changes are planned?*

*What's next? A change of name? Will we become the Cardiff Dragons? Hasn't the example of the local rugby club changing its colours, badge, nickname and ground, yet losing its identity and much of its fan base taught us anything?*

*These plans have pressed ahead without any consultation. Mr Tan, we are glad to have you involved with our football club, but not at the expense of our history. Sam Hammam aired similar ideas but ultimately listened when the club's support objected en masse.*

*Steve Borley, as a man we can trust on the current board of directors, we need you to publically condemn these plans. Malky Mackay, you have united the fans behind you this season and as a man who knows of the importance of tradition at football clubs, we need you to speak out and impress upon our investors that these plans need to be nipped in the bud before it's too late. To the local press, the new Labour led Cardiff Council and our local MPs and AMs, we need you to use whatever influence you can wield to ensure that the traditions of the city's football club are upheld.*

*Now is the time for the various supporters groups, rival message boards and Cardiff fans from all walks of life to unite and ask the football club to come clean about their plans. They need to understand in no uncertain terms that we will not support a re-branded Cardiff City, no matter what the consequences may be. I would rather support my team playing in League Two rather than a team I no longer recognise as my own. Cardiff City play in blue, we are the Bluebirds.*

In 2009, Cardiff's chairman Peter Ridsdale travelled to the Far East to attract investment in the club, which has a substantial long-standing debt with The Langston Corporation, relating to former owner Sam Hammam's reign. Malaysian businessman Dato Chan Tien Ghee was soon added to the club's board and he took over from Ridsdale in May 2010. Vincent Tan, at the time estimated to be worth in excess of $1.3m, has since taken control of the club and subsidised the club's losses without taking any money out of the club. These high-interest loans have kept the threat of administration at bay, but the club continues to make a loss and Tan was keen to implement radical plans to appeal to the Asian market. The club had already released the Cardiff Blues rugby team from their long-term lease at the stadium to enable significant rebranding of the venue; it was now apparent that was just the tip of the iceberg.

The 'leak' resulted from a meeting where the rebrand was revealed, with the added incentive of a £100m sweetener. This would include £6m already invested in equity, £34.8m of loans converted to equity, £10m to pay off Langston, plus a new £10m training complex. Also £12m to increase the Cardiff City Stadium capacity to 35,000, a further £22m of capital expenditure and a substantial transfer fund made available to Mackay. The change was justified in an accompanying statement as an attempt at a "fusion of cultures" between Malaysia and Wales, with red a shared colour and the dragon an important symbol for both countries. Red is also associated with vibrancy, good luck and happiness in the Far East, a royal colour that wards off evil spirits. That Manchester United, Arsenal and Liverpool have prospered in the Asian market, where Chelsea and Manchester City have thus far failed, was also highlighted to emphasise the point.

Fans reacted angrily to the lack of consultation and what they regarded as a cavalier attitude to the club's identity and heritage. Less than 48 hours later, a statement was released revealing that the plans had been shelved due to "vociferous opposition". But there was a caveat; a liberal use of the past tense insinuated that investment would now be scaled back and that interest in the club might cool as a result. Fans began to panic and revise their opinions. Operating an unsustainable business model, the club was losing £1m a month and had an annual wage bill of close to £14m, 88 per cent of the club's turnover. Retaining Tan's interest and involvement was imperative. Chan returned to Cardiff a few days later to discuss matters, but a six-hour meeting failed to resolve the situation and he returned to Malaysia with Cardiff's immediate future in the balance. Within a month plans were revived, the new kit and badge, emblazoned with the new motto, "Fire & Passion", were revealed on 6th June with the following statement.

*On behalf of the board of directors and after constructive and positive discussions with our principal investors, Cardiff City Football Club are delighted to announce that Tan Sri Vincent Tan and Dato Chan Tien Ghee ('our Investor') have pledged their continuing commitment to enable the club to plan for the future. Following a comprehensive review of wider supporter feedback via email, letters, media coverage and polls run via the official Supporters' Club and Media Wales and as a consequence of the above commitment, Cardiff City Football Club will also reactivate rebranding proposals with a view to exploiting and maximising its brand and commercial revenues in international markets, which it is hoped in turn will bring success to the club locally, whilst also attracting new partners and investors.*

During this period, Hammam, who also proposed sweeping changes in 2000, involving a green and white kit with a black and gold Celtic cross on the badge, rejected three offers to clear the Langston debt. The deals on offer were: £8m due within 30 days, £10m with £3m up front and the rest due at the end of the season, or £13m with £8m due this year and £5m if Cardiff were to be promoted. A life presidency was also believed to be on offer but an agreement could not be made, thus restricting the scope of Tan's immediate investment. Mackay also reiterated his commitment to the club, by ruling himself out of the running for the vacant Norwich City management post. Despite the lure of stepping up to the Premier League with his former club, he explained: "I have started a project at Cardiff City, I am fully committed to our club and the challenges ahead." With Cardiff's immediate future secured, he set about spending his considerable transfer budget, ahead of the forthcoming campaign.

Joe Lewis was the first acquisition. The six-foot six-inch, 24-year-old goalkeeper was a free agent after his Peterborough contract expired and he was a former team-mate of Mackay at Norwich. Lewis received a call-up to the senior England squad in May 2008 and was brought in to replace Tom Heaton, who turned down a new contract in favour of regular first-team football at Bristol City. Jordon Mutch was brought in for a fee of around £2m from Birmingham City, who were forced to sell due to their perilous financial state. The powerful England Under-21 international midfielder was a teen prodigy, making his senior debut at 16, but his subsequent development had been hampered by a series of injuries. He enjoyed the most prosperous period of his career to date on loan at Watford, scoring five goals in 23 games under the tutelage of Mackay, so it was no surprise to see the pair reunited.

For his next signings, Mackay highlighted the scope of his scouting network and willingness to recruit from far and wide. Slovakian Under-21 captain Filip Kiss was signed permanently from Slovan Bratislava for £500,000 after impressing on loan at Cardiff with a series of combative performances during the previous season. Highly-rated South Korean Kim Bo-Kyung was also added from Japan's J-League. The versatile attacking midfielder cost around £2m from Cerezo Osaka and is regarded as the heir to Park Ji-sung in the national side. The 22-year-old would join up with Cardiff after the 2012 summer Olympics. Striker Etien Velikonja, a full Slovenian international was brought in for £1.5m to enrich the Cardiff attack, after netting 20 goals in 48 for Maribor. There were also near misses, Fleetwood Town striker Jamie Vardy turned down a £1m move in favour of joining Leicester City, while Coventry rejected an £800,000 bid for centre back Richard Keogh. Cardiff also rejected two bids from Fulham for Peter Whittingham.

After spending pre-season in Switzerland, Cardiff returned at the tail end of July to face **Forest Green Rovers** in their first friendly. Lewis and Velikonja both made their first starts while Mackay fielded a completely different team for the second half. Having trailed 1–0 at the break, that proved to be the only goal of the game, as a lack of match practice saw Cardiff impress only intermittently in defeat. A few days later, they travelled to **Cheltenham Town** and provided a much improved performance. Andrew Taylor, Robert Earnshaw and Craig Conway scored in the first half before Peter Whittingham later added a fourth to secure a 4–0 win.

# Hey big spenders

AUGUST SAW CARDIFF bring in half a dozen new signings, including local hero Craig Bellamy. But despite lavish spending right up to the final moments of the transfer window, City made a stuttering start to the campaign.

4th August – Oxford United (a)
7th August – Bournemouth (a)
11th August – Newcastle United (h)
14th August – Northampton Town (a)
17th August – Huddersfield Town (h)
21st August – Brighton and Hove Albion (a)
25th August – Bristol City (a)

Icelandic veteran Heidur Helguson arrived on 2nd August, a free transfer from QPR after an impressive Premier League campaign with the club. An imposing centre forward, his experience and physicality was sought to replace Kenny Miller and complement the youthful promise of

Mason and Gestede. A few days later, 34-year-old Helguson made his debut in a strong Cardiff side that won 2–1 at **Oxford United**, with goals from Whittingham and Kiss. Helguson's first goal arrived in the subsequent game, another 2–1 win, coming from behind to beat **Bournemouth**, with Whittingham again scoring. Out-of-favour centre back Anthony Gerrard also departed the club for Huddersfield Town.

On 10th August, Cardiff demonstrated their financial muscle with the marquee signing of local hero Craig Bellamy. Born and bred in the area, the prodigal son returned after a year spent with the club during the 2010/11 campaign, a season-long loan from Manchester City. Made captain, he scored eleven goals and provided ten assists in 35 games, with highlights including a 35-yard free kick on his debut against Doncaster Rovers and the winner at fierce rivals Swansea. A hamstring injury sustained in the first leg of the play-offs effectively ended Cardiff's chances of progression to the final, plus the promotion dream that saw Bellamy drop down to the Championship. He joined former club Liverpool ahead of the 2011/12 season, despite a late offer from Cardiff, playing against the Bluebirds in the Carling Cup final later that year.

Signing a two-year deal and taking a

considerable pay cut, Bellamy outlined his desire to end his playing days with Cardiff and help get the club to the top flight. "There is more to life than football and it's important to me to be around my wife and kids and play for Cardiff City." Bellamy also outlined his stance on the rebranding, as fans remained conflicted about recent changes. "The red shirt is fine. I'm sure we would all want Cardiff to stay blue but football changes. As long as there is a Cardiff City Football Club in this city, all will be fine. I would wear pink if I had to. The life and soul of this football club is very important to me. I will be wearing a different colour and that's fine with me."

The signing of Bellamy saw expectations for the upcoming season rocket, ahead of a glamorous home friendly with **Newcastle United**. Bellamy sat out the game against another of his former clubs and Kim Bo-Kyung was also absent, having secured a bronze medal, a place in the Team of the Tournament and military service exemption at the Olympics. Cardiff stunned the visitors, who had finished fifth in the Premier League in the previous season, winning 4–1 with a brace from Gunnarsson, a goal for young prospect Joe Ralls and Velikonja's first for his new club. It was the perfect preparation as they approached their first competitive game of the season, a League Cup tie at **Northampton Town** a few days later.

A combination of Cardiff's first league game, at home to Huddersfield Town, being brought forward to a Friday night for Sky coverage and eight players absent on international duty, saw City field an under-strength side at Sixfields. With 16 players missing, six players made their senior debut, including five teenagers, while fringe players like Dekel Keinan, Stephen McPhail and Craig Conway were drafted in. Cardiff appeared unfazed by the task in hand, taking the lead in only the second minute when Heidur Helguson was bundled over in the area. He converted the resultant penalty, sending the goalkeeper the wrong way. Despite their advantage, Cardiff were unable to take control of the game, as the Cobblers tested Joe Lewis on a number of occasions. Their pressure eventually resulted in an equaliser in the 36th minute, when a long throw found Dave Artell, who made amends for conceding the penalty by heading just inside the post. Northampton themselves took the lead early in the second half, again from a header but this time from a corner. Despite Cardiff's best efforts, the home side drew on their greater experience to hold on to win and advance to the second round.

Having progressed to the final of the

competition a few months earlier, crashing out in the first round was certainly a disappointment, but only Joe Mason had played in both games. Promotion was very much considered the priority and their successful cup run certainly affected their league form, if only because it physically and mentally drained a small squad as the sheer number of games caught up with them. With very little choice regarding the line-up, the elimination was regarded as collateral damage, maybe even a blessing in disguise.

Helguson proved to be the only player selected for both games, as the usual suspects returned for the visit of **Huddersfield**. Malky Mackay's tried and trusted back five of David Marshall, who had recently agreed a new four-year contract, Kevin McNaughton, Ben Turner, Mark Hudson and Andrew Taylor lined up in defence. Peter Whittingham, Don Cowie, Aron Gunnarsson and Jordon Mutch completed the midfield with Craig Bellamy joining Helguson in attack. The first half was underwhelming and the atmosphere was particularly subdued, as fans faced the full force of the rebrand for the first time. Whether the crowd affected the performance or the performance affected the crowd is impossible to ascertain, but the away fans singing "You sold your history" certainly did not help. The Terriers were blunted by the absence of Jordan Rhodes, who scored 39 goals in 39 games during their promotion campaign, but comfortably frustrated their hosts in the early stages. Scott Arfield and Oliver Norwood both had efforts on goal that kept Marshall busy, while Helguson saw a header glance off the bar at the other end.

Cardiff were brighter in the second period, with a penalty appeal ignored plus efforts on goal from Cowie and McNaughton, but were matched every step of the way by Simon Grayson's side. Arfield drew an impressive stop from Marshall before Cardiff finally found a breakthrough in added time. McNaughton lofted the ball in to the box for substitute Joe Mason to head back across goal, Gunnarsson's scuffed effort fell kindly for Hudson who scored from eight yards out. There was just enough time for Huddersfield substitute Anthony Gerrard, making his debut after leaving Cardiff, to become the pantomime villain by cleaning out Filip Kiss near the touchline. The incident earned him a booking and he later remarked on Twitter: "Do you think football is a tickling contest?"

The game ended 1–0, which was harsh on Huddersfield, who did not look out of place competing against one of the pre-season favourites for promotion. Cardiff, meanwhile, were left to reflect on an inauspicious start to the season, which may have yielded three points, but raised more questions than answers. Post-match, Mackay claimed he felt that his side had suffered from opening-night jitters. "Obviously it was a big evening against Huddersfield in terms of the way the summer has gone with the red and blue situation, it was the first game of the season. We had the Malaysian owners over and the game was live here and in Malaysia. It really was the curtain-raiser. There was probably quite a lot of pressure on the players so to keep going was good and it's always nice to score at the end."

On 20th August, QPR accepted Cardiff's £500,000 bid for Matthew Connolly. The versatile 24-year-old defender progressed through the Arsenal academy before joining Rangers in 2008. He had enjoyed back-to-back promotions from the Championship with QPR in 2011 and while on loan at Reading in the following season. Repeating the feat with Cardiff would see him match Mackay's achievement of three-in-a-row. He was a like-for-like replacement for Welsh international Darcy Blake, who had rejected the offer of a new deal at Cardiff and would join Crystal Palace a few days later.

The following day, Cardiff headed to **Brighton**, where they played out a goalless draw with Gus

Poyet's talented Seagulls. Mackay picked an unchanged side and they provided an improved performance against opponents prepared to go toe-to-toe with them. Cardiff nearly took the lead after seven minutes when Mark Hudson rose to head Peter Whittingham's free kick and with Tomasz Kuszczak in the Albion goal beaten, Craig Mackail-Smith was on hand to clear. Andrew Taylor fizzed an effort across goal soon after, only for Heidur Helguson to scoop his effort over the bar. Gradually Brighton gained a foothold in the game, with winger Craig Noone the architect for the home side. Mackay was well aware of Noone's talents, having made a £500,000 bid for the 24-year-old towards the end of the January transfer window in 2012. Without enough time to find a suitable replacement, Cardiff's advances were rebuffed and Noone, instrumental in their promotion from League One as champions in 2011, soon agreed an improved deal with the club.

A Noone cross almost resulted in the equaliser, as Ashley Barnes headed over from close range, before then testing Marshall from distance. Whittingham worked Kuszczak with a 30-yard free kick just before half-time and had a couple of efforts on goal early in the second half. Bruno and Noone brought excellent saves out of Marshall as the end-to-end contest continued, while Kuszczak made a fine double stop from Cardiff substitutes Joe Mason and Etien Velikonja late in the game. A draw was a fair result and Cardiff maintained their unbeaten, albeit underwhelming, start to the season with consecutive clean sheets. Having won eight, drawn eleven and lost only four of their away games in the previous season, it looked as though Malky's men had picked up where they had left off ahead of the forthcoming Severnside derby.

Between fixtures, Mackay brought in another former team-mate in Tommy Smith, formerly of Watford – adept as both a right winger and stationed up front, two positions where Cardiff were lacking depth. The 32-year-old attacker was also the third player signed from QPR, reuniting with Connolly and Helguson. Smith went straight in to the starting line-up for the short trip to **Bristol City**, with Matthew Connolly also making his debut in the heart of the defence, as both Craig Bellamy and Ben Turner were absent with a tight calf and an injured foot respectively.

City started brightly and Smith stung the palms of former Cardiff goalkeeper Tom Heaton early on. Peter Whittingham followed suit soon after, but Bristol began to take control as Cardiff looked uncharacteristically uncomfortable in possession.

As the game passed the 30-minute mark, Bristol's highly-regarded winger Albert Adomah burst past Andrew Taylor on the left flank and centred for Stephen Pearson, who found himself in acres of space twelve yards out to bury the chance past David Marshall. Cardiff almost went in at the break level, when Mark Hudson headed against the bar from a Whittingham corner, but instead Bristol doubled their lead. A punt forward was controlled by Jon Stead, who fed Martyn Woolford to drill in their second.

Joe Mason was introduced at the break for Aron Gunnarsson and his impact was immediate. Another Whittingham set piece, pretty much Cardiff's only attacking outlet, created panic in the Robins defence, with Heaton saving a Helguson header but unable to keep out Mason's follow-up. Despite enjoying a period of sustained pressure, it was Bristol who were to score again. Adomah struck the Cardiff post and Woolford was the quickest to react, converting the rebound for his second goal of the game. Cardiff showed character to respond to this setback, with Helguson reducing the deficit from close range with eight minutes left, but Bristol ended any hope of a comeback in injury time, as debutant Sam Baldock broke forward to net a decisive fourth.

After three games, Cardiff had won one, lost one

and drawn one, mid-table form which displayed some of the deficiencies from the previous season. A chronic lack of width remained. Don Cowie is capable of filling in on the wing, but is not a winger by trade. A fierce work ethic is his great strength, but he has a tendency to drift inside and lacks the pace and trickery to beat a full back, while Craig Conway remained out of favour. Craig Bellamy has a knee problem which requires micro-managing and is unable to play every game, while Tommy Smith was still adapting to his new surroundings. They had also lost leads in two of their first four games, a regular occurrence in their first season under Mackay. In the previous campaign, losing a lead on 13 occasions had cost them 31 potential points.

Fortunately, the first problem was soon addressed, as Craig Noone signed in a £1m deal on 30th August, while Peter Whittingham also agreed a new deal, his third during Mackay's reign. Cardiff completed their summer spending with 30 minutes of the transfer window remaining, agreeing a £2.5m deal for West Ham United striker Nicky Maynard. Prolific for Crewe Alexandra and Bristol City earlier in his career, 25-year-old Maynard was a fringe player at West Ham. He scored in the second leg of the play-offs against Cardiff, but found he was even further down the pecking order when the Hammers returned to the Premier League. In total, Cardiff had spent in excess of £10m during the summer and the squad boasted far greater strength in depth as a result. Despite a wealth of options in most areas, the defence looked a little bit low on numbers, with only Connolly added while Darcy Blake, Anthony Gerrard, Dekel Keinan, Paul Quinn and Lee Naylor all departed. With only five senior defenders remaining, any injuries sustained could seriously compromise Cardiff's prospects.

# Malky's men find their feet

CARDIFF'S NEW SIGNINGS combined to great effect in September to propel City up the table, as questions were raised regarding the well-being of one new arrival, while another sustained a potentially season-ending injury.

2nd September – Wolves (h)
15th September – Leeds United (h)
18th September – Millwall (a)
22nd September – Crystal Palace (a)
29th September – Blackpool (h)

Cardiff soon banished any talk of a stuttering start to the season, commencing September in blistering fashion by comprehensively beating **Wolves** 3–1 and recording a second consecutive home win. Cardiff handed debuts to Craig Noone and Nicky Maynard, while both Tommy Smith and Matthew Connolly made their home bow. Craig Bellamy and Ben Turner were both still absent. The game started at a frenetic pace, with Noone demonstrating the pace and trickery that had been lacking in previous games. Wolves goalkeeper Carl Ikeme did well to keep out his fierce effort on six minutes, but Wolves soon took the lead, against the run of play. A Peter Whittingham shove on Sylvan Ebanks-Blake saw Wolves, a Premier League side a few months earlier, awarded a free kick on the edge of the box. Bakary Sako slammed his effort past David Marshall to open the scoring, but City were level less than 60 seconds later. Again Noone was the architect, breaking into the box and drawing the foul from Ronald Zubar, as Whittingham equalised from the penalty spot. Maynard was heavily involved in the second, collecting the ball on the edge of the area, squaring to Jordon Mutch, who allowed the ball to run through his legs for Whittingham to fire Cardiff in to the lead, the third goal in the opening 15 minutes.

Cardiff lined up in a 4–4–2 formation, to utilise both Maynard and Heidur Helguson up front. The change of shape gave them a better balance, provided far greater attacking options and set up an intriguing contrast with Stale Solbakken's compact 4–5–1. It proved to be an even contest as the half progressed, with David Edwards and Sako both forcing decent saves from Marshall. Noone almost extended Cardiff's lead before half-time, with a mazy run from inside his own penalty area to force a good save from Ikeme. He also turned a Whittingham free kick around the post in the second half, denying him a hat-trick, but he was merely postponing the feat. A Tongo Doumbia foul on Noone in the 66th minute, resulted in Cardiff's number seven bending an effort in to the top corner to secure the three points and the match ball. Noone was replaced in the 74th minute and received a standing ovation for his dazzling debut performance, which ensured that Cardiff went in to the international break in fine form.

Malky Mackay spent the break reassuring everyone that Craig Bellamy remained committed to the Cardiff cause, after a number of rumours surfaced regarding his continued absence from the team. Accusations that issues in his personal life were behind his lack of appearances were dismissed, and a torn calf was confirmed. Having also withdrawn from international duty, Mackay explained: "Initially, we thought he would be back for us against Wolves on Sunday, but the scans have shown that he's nowhere near it. It's certainly going to be at least Leeds." Addressing the speculation, he added: "There are plenty of rumours going about, but I've told you he's torn his calf." An interview with Bellamy in the *Sunday Mirror* a few days later confirmed that, injury aside, his personal life was also in turmoil. He revealed that he was still struggling to come to terms with the death of his best friend and international manager Gary Speed, that it had cost him his marriage and that he "couldn't give a shit about football". Suggestions that he was set to retire from football were dismissed, but he did concede that he was experiencing "the worst time in my life ever".

Bellamy did return for the visit of **Leeds**, but was deemed only fit enough for a place on the bench, as Mackay fielded an unchanged side. Neil Warnock was forced to shuffle his pack when former Cardiff forward Ross McCormack twisted his ankle after only three minutes. A typically physical first half with very few chances ensued. Heidur Helguson wasted the best opportunity, heading a Peter Whittingham cross over the bar from close range. Cardiff improved after the break, stretching play and utilising their strength in wide areas as Nicky Maynard and Mark Hudson both had efforts repelled by Paddy Kenny. Craig Noone was withdrawn after 64 minutes, as Bellamy entered proceedings to the delight of the home support. A few minutes later, they were on their feet again to salute Bellamy as he fired Cardiff in to the lead, with a free kick drilled from the edge of the area.

The goal succeeded in opening up the game and the lead was soon doubled when Maynard was clumsily brought down in the area by Tom Lees. Whittingham sent Kenny the wrong way with his penalty. Leeds gave themselves a chance of an unlikely recovery when Rodolph Austin scored a 30-yard free kick which, hit towards the centre of his goal, Marshall will have been disappointed to concede. Kenny kept Leeds in contention with a couple of late saves from Maynard and Tommy Smith, but Cardiff were fortunate to hold on for the win, as Lee Peltier headed just over the bar late on, with Marshall beaten. Post-match, Mackay revealed his delight at the improved second-half performance, explaining: "We had 19 chances at goal and Paddy Kenny made three or four magnificent saves. On another day we could have scored four or five." With three points in the bag, attention now turned to the following weekend's trip to The New Den to face Millwall.

With Bellamy rested, Aron Gunnarsson was drafted in to midfield as Heidur Helguson dropped to the bench and Cardiff reverted to a 4–5–1 formation, with Nicky Maynard as the sole forward. **Millwall** shaded the early exchanges, as a James Henry chance was blocked by a last-ditch Andrew Taylor tackle. Whittingham found the net after 21 minutes, bending a 25-yard free kick past the helpless Maik Taylor, only to see it harshly ruled out for a seemingly insignificant shirt-pulling incident between Gunnarsson and Jimmy Abdou. Jordon Mutch soon went close, heading a Kevin McNaughton cross wide of the post, while Keyleigh Osbourne and Henry were both denied by David Marshall at the other end as the half ended goalless. Once again, the Bluebirds improved in the second half and took control of the game with two goals in two minutes. Craig Noone slid a pass across the penalty area for Whittingham to score his fifth goal of the season before Noone himself extended the lead, bending an effort just inside the post from 15 yards. The winger was later substituted for Kim Bo-Kyung, making his debut for the club with a brief cameo appearance.

With Mark Hudson and Matthew Connolly providing a formidable barrier in defence, as Tommy Smith and Noone kept the Millwall defence on their toes, Cardiff never looked like relinquishing their lead and the result cemented them in the top six. But the result was tarnished by a serious injury sustained by Maynard.

Catching his studs in the turf, he twisted his knee and appeared in great discomfort as he left the field. It was later confirmed that he had torn his anterior cruciate ligament and would miss the rest of the season, a devastating blow for both Maynard and the club, after a bright start to his career in South Wales following his recent move. Having previously recovered from a similar injury to his other knee in 2010, Maynard has prior experience of the frustration and lengthy rehabilitation process involved. "I'm devastated," Maynard revealed, "three games in I get an injury like I have and I'm out for six to nine months. Now I've got it in my head that I'm not going to play again this season, if I do then it's a bonus."

Despite Maynard's absence, Robert Earnshaw was allowed to leave the club on a season-long loan to Israeli outfit Maccabi Tel Aviv on 20th September. The 31-year-old returned to his former club in July 2011 after scoring 105 goals in 205 games for them earlier in his career, before a £3m move to West Bromwich Albion in 2004. He scored three times in his second spell, before being largely frozen out of the side from October onwards, deemed incompatible with first-choice striker Kenny Miller. The only player to score a hat-trick in every domestic competition and international level, where he earned 58 caps for

Wales, he was very much on the periphery during the current campaign. An unused substitute against Huddersfield, Brighton and Bristol City, he was now considered expendable, to the delight of Maccabi's sports director Jordi Cruyff.

Cardiff headed to **Crystal Palace** with designs on a fourth successive win and their best start to a league season since the 1950s. Unfortunately, things did not go according to plan. Craig Bellamy started in place of Craig Noone, who had been in impressive form, while Don Cowie and Aron Gunnarsson combined in central midfield. Their influence was to prove significant in the first half, as City once again benefited from two goals scored in quick succession. With 13 minutes played, Gunnarsson strode through midfield before playing a neat one-two with fellow Icelander Heidur Helguson, benefiting from a lucky bounce off a Palace defender before dispatching past Julián Speroni. A trademark Gunnarsson long throw led to the second, as Bellamy's effort on goal was partially blocked but spun in to the path of Cowie who added a second. A few minutes later, Bellamy spurned a golden chance to make it three, firing over from ten yards out.

Cardiff held a 2–0 lead at half-time, but not for long. After 51 minutes, they conceded a penalty in controversial circumstances, as an André

Moritz free kick struck an arm in the wall. It was questionable whether or not there was any intent involved but Glenn Murray casually converted the penalty all the same. Ten minutes later Palace equalised in calamitous circumstances, as a Jonathan Parr shot deflected off Mark Hudson, which fell kindly to Murray who diverted it towards goal as both David Marshall and Matthew Connolly failed to prevent the effort from crossing the line. Dougie Freedman's men eventually took the lead when Helguson mistimed a challenge to upend Parr and concede a second penalty. The challenge appeared to be just outside the box, but Murray sealed his hat-trick from the spot and an unlikely 3–2 win.

The result left Cardiff sixth, three points behind leaders Brighton, as Malky Mackay reflected on what might have been. "I'm disappointed. If we had not given the two penalties we would be sitting near the top of the table. But there's no need to overreact. We know exactly where we went wrong, we committed suicide really by gifting Crystal Palace two penalties."

Cowie echoed the sentiment, adding: "I'm gutted. We let ourselves down, simple as that."

Having bounced back from the defeat against Bristol City by embarking on a three-game winning streak, Cardiff were looking to commence another run starting with their final September fixture, at home to **Blackpool**. Craig Noone returned to the starting line-up at the expense of Don Cowie and Cardiff received a pre-match boost as Blackpool's star performer Thomas Ince missed the trip with an injury. A bright opening saw Craig Bellamy and Blackpool's Matt Phillips, a former City transfer target, go close early on. Matthew Connolly netted the opening goal from a Bellamy cross on 17 minutes and Peter Whittingham made it 2–0 with yet another free kick ten minutes later. There was to be no dramatic revival from the opposition this time though, as Connolly headed in a Bellamy corner just before the hour to put the game out of reach for the visitors. Phillips hit a post and Stephen Crainey hit the crossbar in injury time as Blackpool tried to reduce the deficit, but the game ended 3–0 and Cardiff moved up to second in the table. The only negative aspect of the game was Tommy Smith limping off after 25 minutes with a hamstring injury. Malky Mackay claimed that the result was his side's "best performance of the season", while the Tangerines manager Ian Holloway insisted that Cardiff "won't score easier goals in their lives than those they got against us".

# Cardiff take to the front

CARDIFF'S FORMIDABLE FORM continued in October with a couple of late wins and a comprehensive victory, but patchy away form remained a concern.

2nd October – Birmingham City (h)
6th October – Ipswich Town (a)
20th October – Nottingham Forest (a)
23rd October – Watford (h)
27th October – Burnley (h)

A few days after their impressive showing against Blackpool, Cardiff entertained **Birmingham City** on a soaking wet Tuesday night, facing a team wearing blue for the first time in their new red home kit. A hard fought 2–1 victory saw the Bluebirds match a 66-year-old feat with regards to their formidable home form, recording their fifth consecutive win. They also topped the Championship for the first time, one point ahead of fellow big spenders Leicester City. Joe Mason started in place of Tommy Smith and Cardiff struggled to create chances in dreadful conditions against a disciplined Birmingham side that enjoyed the better chances early on. David Marshall did well to keep out a Leroy Lita header on 15 minutes and the striker, on loan from Swansea City, also wasted another great chance with wayward shooting. Six minutes before the break, Cardiff made the most of their first real opportunity, when Mark Hudson squared a Peter Whittingham cross for Craig Bellamy to stroke home from close range. After a tussle with Hudson, which earned a free kick in a dangerous position, Lita swept in Wade Elliott's delivery to level the contest early in the second half. Hudson made amends three minutes later, converting Whittingham's cross to restore his side's one-goal lead. Bellamy, Aron Gunnarsson and Birmingham sub Marlon King all had late chances but Cardiff secured the win ahead of a long trip to struggling **Ipswich** the following weekend.

Craig Bellamy did not make the journey, having been substituted late in the Birmingham match in order to rest his knees after playing twice in the space of four games. His exertions also saw him once again withdraw from international duty, much to the disappointment of Chris Coleman. As a result, he issued Bellamy with an ultimatum regarding his future in the national side. Don Cowie took his place in the side, with Joe Mason playing up front alongside Heidur Helguson. Despite not recording a win in eight Championship matches, it was Ipswich that took the upper hand in the first half, as Aaron Cresswell's cross was volleyed over the bar by on-loan striker DJ Campbell. Jay Emmanuel-Thomas, who had spent the season on loan with Cardiff a couple of years earlier, forced David Marshall in to a fine save and a Daryl Murphy header also struck the crossbar. The Tractor Boys took a deserved lead just before half-time, but the goal should not have counted, as Campbell diverted Lee Martin's cross in to the back of the net quite blatantly with his hand. The misdemeanour was missed and the goal stood.

With Cardiff trailing and struggling on the road once again, a big second-half performance was required if they were to retain top spot. The introduction of Craig Conway, making only his second appearance of the season, certainly upped the tempo and provided more cutting edge. It was a Conway cross that led to the equaliser, as goalkeeper Scott Loach spilled the ball in to the path of Helguson, for an easy tap in. Rudy Gestede, having recently returned to full fitness, replaced Mason and added a more direct attacking outlet up front. His shot from the edge of the area led to a late Cardiff winner, as his effort found its way to Andrew Taylor on the left who crossed for Helguson to notch his and Cardiff's second with only two minutes remaining. The veteran forward headed against his own bar soon after but City held on for a morale-boosting away win. Helguson's fine performance was also timely, as fans had begun to criticise his continued selection after six games without a goal.

Malky Mackay was keen to praise him post-match, claiming: "Heidar ended up running himself dizzy at the end and I think he is a credit to the profession. People were beginning to question him not being on the scoresheet, but the amount of energy, work rate and passion he puts in is incredible. He is a credit to himself and someone the youngsters should look up to because he's a proven Premier League goal-scorer, proven international footballer and at 35 is still chasing the ball to earn us a corner in the last minute of the game. He is still scoring headers and also scoring tap-ins by being in the right place at the right time and right now he is sitting in a bath of ice!"

If Cardiff had thought they had turned a corner regarding their form away from home, they were very much mistaken, as their worst performance yet was just around the corner. The following weekend they travelled to the City Ground to face **Nottingham Forest** and were this time on the receiving end of a two-goal, two-minute blitz. On 24 minutes, Kevin McNaughton brought down Andy Reid on the edge of the box. The Irish international took the free kick and his effort curled past David Marshall and in off the crossbar. Before they had chance to regroup, Forest had doubled their lead through Daniel Ayala. Greg Halford whipped in an inviting cross from the right and Ayala beat his markers to power the cross into the back of the net. With Bellamy once again absent and Craig Conway underwhelming, after earning a first start due to his impressive Ipswich showing, a ballooned Heidur Helguson effort was all Cardiff had to show for their first-half toil. Sluggish and short of ideas, despite a two-week break since their last game, Mackay's men were three goals down within two minutes of the restart. Forest substitute Radoslaw Majewski split the Cardiff defence to feed Billy Sharp, who calmly slotted past Marshall. City gradually improved, as Don Cowie and Mark Hudson both saw efforts go narrowly wide of Lee Camp's goal. They eventually reduced the deficit when Helguson headed in from a Rudy Gestede high ball, but it was too little, too late. Tommy Smith also hit a post and Adlène Guedioura was sent off for two bookable offences, but the game ended 3–1 as Cardiff's struggles on the road continued and Leicester leapfrogged them in the table.

Cardiff returned to winning ways in a midweek encounter with **Watford**, but needed to come from behind against nine men to do so, with a last-minute winner. Mackay made three changes for the visit of Gianfranco Zola's side, Ben Turner returned in place of Kevin McNaughton, as Matthew Connolly moved across to right back. Craig Bellamy replaced Craig Conway, while Craig Noone was brought in at the expense of Aron Gunnarsson, as Don Cowie occupied a berth in central midfield. Bellamy felt the effects of a robust Marco Cassetti challenge early on and required lengthy treatment on his ankle, but was able to continue. The Italian veteran was then booked for a tackle on Noone and also later warned regarding further offences. It proved to be a sign of things to come, but not before Watford had taken the lead. With almost half-an-hour of the first half played, a Mark Yeates corner was met by Cassetti who forced David Marshall to make a fine save, only for Tommy Hoban to convert the rebound. Cowie and Tommy Smith had attempts on the Watford goal, but Cardiff trailed at the interval and Bellamy's ankle was unable to sustain a further 45 minutes. He did not re-emerge for the second period and was replaced by Joe Mason.

As Watford defended the lead deep in their own half, City struggled to create chances and the Hornets remained a threat on the break, with a Fitz Hall shot clipping Marshall's bar. After 64 minutes, Watford were reduced to ten men when Daniel Pudil lashed out at Noone and they conceded a penalty soon after when Connolly's shot struck Jonathan Hogg's arm. It looked a harsh decision, but Peter Whittingham dutifully converted from twelve yards for his seventh goal of the season. Mere minutes later, Nathaniel Chalobah received a second yellow card for foolishly kicking the ball away and Cardiff responded by withdrawing centre back Turner in favour of another striker in Rudy Gestede. Gunnarsson also replaced Smith late on and it was the Icelandic international who earned the win, heading in a Noone cross in injury time. A record-breaking sixth consecutive win had been secured. Zola was left to reflect on a "very cruel" result, but a patient Cardiff capitalised on Watford's indiscipline.

The late win saw Cardiff approach their weekend fixture with **Burnley** in an upbeat fashion with a new loan signing in tow. Talented 18-year-old Fulham winger Kerim Frei was brought in on a one-month deal as cover for Craig Bellamy and Tommy Smith, who were both withdrawn in the previous game. Frei was among the substitutes as Kim Bo-Kyung made his first start and made an instant impact. In only the third minute, Kim fed Craig Noone on the right who cut inside on to his left foot and struck the post with a curling effort. Joe Mason reacted quickest to the rebound and had the luxury of a few touches before firing past Lee Grant. Charlie Austin, who had already netted 15 goals for the Clarets, hooked a volley that had David Marshall scurrying to keep out, before a Mason effort then struck a post. Kim fired just wide of goal and Heidur Helguson wasted a headed opportunity before the Bluebirds finally increased their lead. Noone let rip from 25 yards as the interval approached and Grant did well to get a hand on the dipping effort, but not a good enough hand as the ball crept over the line before he could scoop it clear. Cardiff were well on top and thoroughly deserved their lead, attacking with pace and pressing the opposition consistently. Ben Turner saw a diving header clear the bar ten minutes into the second half and Noone once again struck the woodwork, cutting in from the right and bending his shot against the bar. With eight minutes remaining, Matthew Connolly was left unmarked to head in Peter Whittingham's cross, just before Frei replaced man-of-the-match Noone, to make his debut. Super-sub Aron Gunnarsson added a fourth, converting from Rudy Gestede's cushioned header as Cardiff returned to the Championship summit in style, three points clear of Leicester.

Mackay singled out Noone for praise after the game, explaining: "Craig was someone we looked at for a number of years. We tried to bring him to Watford and we tried to tempt him out of Brighton in January, but the situation in the summer allowed us to get him and I feel there's a lot more potential to get out of him. He's come into football by a slightly different route [non-league] but he's got bags of personality and has a huge talent to start with. He wants to learn and playing with good players rubs off as well."

After what he described as the team's most complete performance to date, he also lauded the unity within the squad. "The players and everyone else at the club have shown a great togetherness but I'm acutely aware of this division, everything in it and how relentless and unforgiving it is. Teams can quickly be decimated with injuries, we've seen that ourselves with Nicky Maynard, Craig Bellamy, Jordon Mutch and Tommy Smith, four players we've brought into the group. So I'm delighted with the guys who have stepped in, taken places and grabbed the jerseys. They are making it difficult for others to get them back."

Two of the players on the outside looking in were Kevin McNaughton and Etien Velikonja. McNaughton had lost his place as a result of the return of Ben Turner and a poor showing in the limp defeat at Nottingham Forest. But Mackay was full of admiration for the attitude of the 30-year-old full back, who had spent six years with the club and represented Scotland at international level. He described him as a top professional, always pushing for a starting place and ready when needed. Velikonja, adapting to a new country and culture, also admitted that he was enduring a frustrating period in South Wales. "It is true that I have played less than I expected," the Slovenian international revealed. "When I arrived in Cardiff, it was all excellent. I played in all the matches before the start of the season, I scored a goal at Newcastle United, but then it all changed. When I got back from Slovenia duty, I moved to the bench. I cannot be satisfied, but my position is not alarming yet."

# Home comforts and away-day blues

ADEMORALISING DEFEAT proves to be a pivotal moment in November, as Cardiff top the table by matching their best ever sequence of home wins.

3rd November – Bolton Wanderers (a)
6th November – Charlton Athletic (a)
10th November – Hull City (h)
17th November – Middlesbrough (h)
24th November – Barnsley (a)
27th November – Derby County (a)

On 2nd November, Cardiff announced the appointment of Dick Bate as the club's new academy manager, replacing Neal Ardley who left the post to take charge at AFC Wimbledon. The experienced coach vacated a high-profile role as the FA's elite coaching director and would oversee every age group from under-nines through to under-21s. After 13 games, Cardiff had won all seven of their home fixtures but had lost three of their six encounters away from home. With their fortunes at the Cardiff City Stadium likely to recede to some extent in the future, the onus was on finding greater consistency on their travels, as a tough trip to **Bolton Wanderers** approached. In the days leading up to the game, Malky Mackay had to address claims that Cardiff lacked ambition away from home, but he dismissed the accusation, instead citing individual errors. Dougie Freedman would be in charge of Bolton for the first time, having left Crystal Palace to replace former Wanderers boss Owen Coyle. There is no love lost between Freedman and the Cardiff fans after he claimed they were "scared stiff of failure" ahead of the previous season's Carling Cup final. Despite losing that battle of wits, he had masterminded Palace's remarkable comeback from two goals down to win 3–2 back in September and he was to repeat the feat again, albeit in far less dramatic fashion.

The first half was largely uneventful until Cardiff, fielding an unchanged side, took the lead just before half-time. A Peter Whittingham cross caused panic in the Bolton defence and Zat Knight failed to clear his lines. Craig Noone's effort on goal crept past Knight, Stephen Warnock and the unsighted Ádám Bogdán in goal to give Mackay's side the advantage. But the introduction of Martin Petrov and especially David N'Gog early in the second half changed the game. N'Gog soon had a perfectly good goal disallowed but won a penalty for his side when Kim Bo-Kyung was adjudged to have tripped him. The decision was harsh as he looked to have already been on his way to ground before the challenge, but Petrov made no mistake from the spot with 20 minutes remaining. Five minutes later, N'Gog flicked a Sam Ricketts shot past David Marshall from six yards out. There was late drama when Mark Hudson was bundled to the ground by Warnock in the Bolton penalty area but the incident was not penalised. Marshall, in the opposition box for a set-piece, also saw his attempt cannon off Bogdan's face, as Bolton held on to win.

Mackay chastised the officials, stating on TV: "Do I feel hard done by? In a word, yes. I certainly hope the referee and the linesman look at their performances because neither of them were good enough tonight." His frustration was understandable, but if the officiating was poor, it was poor for both sides. The cold, hard truth was that, despite being top, seven points from seven away games was a poor return and alarm bells were ringing after losing three of their last four games on the road. Craig Noone also jumped to the team's defence, claiming: "I don't think the performances are that bad away from home. We keep hearing that we win our home games, but we are not that good away. I think that's rubbish because the performances have been there away from home as well, it's just been the results."

Three days later, it went from bad to worse. Cardiff travelled to The Valley to face **Charlton Athletic**, reigning League One champions but still finding their feet in the Championship, having lost their last three games at home. Cardiff took control of the contest after only four minutes, as Heidur Helguson glanced in a Peter Whittingham corner. Another Whittingham corner on 24 minutes was flicked on by Mark Hudson for Ben Turner who headed against the bar, with Joe Mason converting the rebound. But six minutes before half-time, the usually dependable David Marshall spilled a cross, allowing Johnnie Jackson to halve the deficit. In injury time, Rob Hulse rounded the keeper and Turner blocked his effort, conceding a corner from which Jackson equalised with an unchallenged header. Nine minutes after the break, the Addicks won a free kick 30 yards out and with everyone expecting a cross, Dale

Stephens managed to loft it over Marshall to give Charlton the lead. Then five minutes later, Bradley Pritchard set up Danny Haynes for a close-range fourth before veteran target man Rob Hulse rose to head in Charlton's fifth, with 25 minutes still to play.

Cardiff were reeling but, in fairness, they managed to stem the flow of pressure and even netted two injury time consolation goals to make the result more respectable. Noone rounded Ben Hamer to score and Aron Gunnarsson also fired in from close range, but there was no disguising their complete collapse. Mackay later admitted that there had been a forthright exchange of views in the dressing room after the game, but considered that to be positive. Both Marshall and Hudson were singled out for criticism, but Mackay provided a staunch defence of both players, outlining their importance and quality. "My goalkeeper has been nothing short of exceptional during the time I've been here. I would not swap him for anyone in the Championship." He added: "Hudson is a fantastic captain, make no mistake about that, whilst I have been here he has been absolutely exceptional." But he did concede that shipping five goals was "unforgiveable" and that too many players had an "off-night". Fortunately, Cardiff could look forward to home comforts as their next two games, against Hull City and Middlesbrough, were back in South Wales.

Against Steve Bruce's **Hull**, Kevin McNaughton returned to the side in place of the absent Matthew Connolly and Kerim Frei, who started against Charlton, dropped to the bench to be replaced by Kim Bo-Kyung. It was business as usual back at the Cardiff City Stadium, as the home side made another swift start. Heidur Helguson bravely headed in a Craig Noone cross at the far post and required lengthy treatment before he could continue. City fashioned plenty of chances, as a Hudson header struck the bar, while Joe Mason and Aron Gunnarsson both went close. As half-time approached, Hull striker Jay Simpson had a goal harshly disallowed by a marginal offside call. Cardiff continued to create openings in the second half, as Ben Amos denied Noone and Peter Whittingham drew an excellent save. Sone Aluko clipped the bar with a 25-yard free kick and Whittingham followed suit from even further out. Mark Hudson eventually doubled City's lead with a header eight minutes from time, a fair reflection of their dominance, only for Robert Koren to net a long-range volley in added time. The 2–1 win put three points between the sides, with Cardiff in third and Hull fourth.

A week later, Cardiff were looking to equal a

club record of nine wins in a row, set in 1951 and again in 2000. Ahead of the arrival of second-placed **Middlesbrough**, Andrew Taylor, formerly of Boro, agreed a two-year contract extension. Regarding his new deal, which will run through to the end of the 2015/16 season, Taylor said: "I needed no persuasion at all to extend my contract. I am very happy here and enjoying my football at a big club." Mackay praised his trusted left back by commenting that: "He has been extremely consistent in terms of ability on the ball, defending and his overall game. He is a great lad with a great temperament and work ethic, as well as a will to do well and work hard." Having signed him on loan at Watford, Mackay brought him to Cardiff in July 2011 when his Middlesbrough contract expired. The former England Under-21 international has been an automatic first choice ever since and lined up against his former club as Cardiff secured a hard fought 1–0 win.

The match saw five players substituted with injuries. Three for Cardiff, including two within the first 30 minutes, and two for Middlesbrough. The first of which was Ben Turner, replaced by academy graduate and debutant Ben Nugent, then Taylor hobbled off, deputised by young prospect Joe Ralls. With Kevin McNaughton already sidelined and a lack of cover at left back,

Aron Gunnarsson dropped back from midfield to fill in. Between these changes, Matthew Connolly scored the only goal of the game, as an excellent Peter Whittingham delivery presented him with the easiest of headers. Scott McDonald and Lukas Jutkiewicz both had chances for the visitors and Emmanuel Ledesma struck the Cardiff bar from a free kick, with David Marshall beaten. Whittingham tested Luke Steele with a low free kick and Craig Bellamy replaced the injured Gunnarsson on the hour, as Ralls deputised in defence. Despite the disruptions, Cardiff clinched all three points and a clean sheet, leapfrogging Boro in to second position, two points behind leaders Crystal Palace.

In the midst of an injury crisis, Mackay moved swiftly in the transfer market to bring in experienced full back Simon Lappin from Norwich City on loan. Signed on 21st November, the 29-year-old would go straight in to the squad for the upcoming trip to **Barnsley**. A regular in the Norwich side that secured back-to-back promotions from League One to reach the Premier League, he had played very little during the current campaign under new boss Chris Hughton. The next day, Kerim Frei was also recalled by parent club Fulham after making three appearances for the Bluebirds. Craig Conway, who had played the same number of games as the departing Frei, also had a transfer request rejected. The former Dundee United winger was Mackay's first signing for the club but was largely out of favour since the arrival of several wingers in the summer and was keen to engineer a move elsewhere. Mackay clarified the situation by stating that Craig had put in a transfer request which had been refused, adding, "He will not be leaving in January unless something drastic happens."

He took his place on the bench at Oakwell, as Ben Nugent made his first start for the club and Simon Lappin made his debut. With 22 minutes on the clock, Nugent rose highest to head a Peter Whittingham corner past Luke Steele in the Barnsley goal, the twelfth time in 18 games that Cardiff had taken the lead. A few minutes later, Lappin was lucky to escape with a yellow card for a reckless lunge on Jonathan Greening. The Tykes wasted a couple of decent chances in the first half, with Stephen Dawson slicing a chance and Marcus Tudgay heading wide from a few yards out, but opportunities for both sides were few and far between. Six minutes after the break, Aron Gunnarsson converted a close-range header from another Whittingham corner to extend the Cardiff lead and ease the away-day jitters of their supporters. But almost inevitably, City invited Barnsley back in to the game. A Jacob Mellis cross eluded everyone to find the back of the Cardiff net with 15 minutes remaining; then Lappin was dismissed after a second booking. Despite a late Barnsley rally, Mackay's men did not buckle and earned a gritty away win.

Much of the praise was reserved for 19-year-old Nugent, a few days shy of his 20th birthday. His emergence had been an unexpected bonus and eased a defensive crisis that would have been far more grave without him. Mackay regards him as a future Cardiff captain and his current partner in defence, Mark Hudson, confirmed that he concurs with his manager's appraisal. "I would have to agree with the gaffer's assessment that Ben will one day be Cardiff skipper, but not for a few years yet," Hudson quipped. "The great thing about him is that he has a real willingness to learn every day. He's pretty quiet and he keeps himself to himself really, but he's always listening and very quick to pick up on things. He's done brilliantly to come in to the side and do so well so quickly. There's no doubt if he carries on in the way he is now he's got a big future in the game."

As a 17-year-old, Nugent was actually released by the club, after a series of injuries had disrupted his development. Academy chief Neal

Ardley invited Nugent to continue training with the youth team and he was eventually rewarded with a new contract. He now also captains the under-21 side. Nugent retained his place for the Tuesday night trip to **Derby County** a few days later, with Joe Ralls required to cover at left back and Craig Bellamy returning to the starting line-up, stationed up front with Heidur Helguson.

Derby had the better of the opening exchanges and captain Richard Keogh, a pre-season Cardiff target, had an early header cleared off the line. But almost inevitably, it was Cardiff that took the lead. Mark Hudson had his header tipped on to the bar by Adam Legzdins and Heidur Helguson was on hand to nod in his seventh goal of the season. Michael Jacobs shot wide for the home side and Paul Coutts drew a fine save from David Marshall as the half drew to a close. Lappin's dismissal at Oakwell was the first Cardiff red card in two years and, remarkably, a second City player received his marching orders in the space of a few days at Pride Park. Craig Noone was shown two yellow cards in the space of three minutes midway through the second half – but where Cardiff were able to see out the Barnsley game, this time they conceded their advantage. Craig Bryson broke in to the Cardiff box and provided Theo Robinson with a simple tap in to level the score with 20 minutes remaining. It was backs to the wall from the Cardiff defence, as full back John Brayford went close on a couple of occasions. A Derby penalty appeal was waved away and a Nathan Tyson header was cleared off the line by Matthew Connolly in injury time, as Cardiff demonstrated defensive steel that had been lacking in recent away performances. The point was also enough to keep them one point ahead of Crystal Palace at the top of the Championship.

DECEMBER

# Festive cheer

A FAMILIAR FACE returned in December, as Cardiff impressed during a congested festive period. Away form significantly improved but their proud unbeaten record came to an end after a shock defeat.

2nd December – Sheffield Wednesday (h)
7th December – Blackburn Rovers (a)
15th December – Peterborough United (h)
22nd December – Leicester City (a)
26th December – Crystal Palace (h)
29th December – Millwall (h)

Cardiff's first December fixture saw the return of former manager Dave Jones, with his struggling **Sheffield Wednesday** side. Having lost their previous five games, Jones was keen to end that run and added spice to the occasion by alluding to a certain enduring issue with his old club. "I've got a problem with them that will come to light eventually," he revealed, refusing to elaborate further. The assumption was that he was still owed money by the club, relating to his 2011 sacking. He received a muted reception when he emerged from the tunnel, greeted by his successor and adversary for the afternoon. Cardiff made four changes for the Sunday clash, as Ben Turner, Andrew Taylor and Jordon Mutch all returned from injury, while Craig Conway replaced the suspended Craig Noone. Craig Bellamy created an early opportunity for Taylor but the Bluebirds failed to make the most of a succession of corners against a big, physical Wednesday side. With five in midfield, the Owls were content to soak up pressure and hit their hosts on the break, as substitute Gary Madine saw his effort saved by David Marshall when he was put clean through. Joe Mason and Rudy Gestede were introduced and the former soon headed a good chance just wide. Cardiff eventually made the breakthrough when Wednesday only half-cleared a ball into the box, Conway controlled with his knee before firing a left-foot drive just inside Chris Kirkland's far post. A few late corners failed to trouble the Cardiff defence and they claimed their tenth home win, a new club record.

Malky Mackay was keen to praise the decisive contribution of Conway, who made his first league start. "This season Craig Conway has worked hard at training. He has had to wait for chances and when Noone came out of the team because of suspension he stepped in and showed he can make an impact. That's exactly what we wanted to see from him. Players go in and do well. That means they hold the jersey at that point." Meanwhile Conway was also delighted to be able to make a positive contribution, after seeing a recent transfer request rejected.

Cardiff headed to Ewood Park for a televised Friday night fixture with Mackay in a reflective mood, praising a core group of players he has depended on in his side's ascent to the top of the league. "There are four or five guys: Peter Whittingham, David Marshall, Matt Connolly, Mark Hudson and more, who have been mainstays of the team in the period when we had injuries hit us. They are just good professionals who turn up every week, play to a certain standard and train to make sure their body is right for an arduous 46-game season and they do that year after year after year. They are guys who are gold dust, the guys you want in your team and in your club. Every club is looking for those guys, those model consistent professionals. It's not an easy thing to do when you think of the amount of stress they are putting on their bodies every two or three days for a long period of time. You get four or five players like that in the team then it's a great spine to any club."

Don Cowie and Craig Noone both returned to the side to face **Blackburn**, with new Rovers boss Henning Berg aiming for a first home win. The opening exchanges were closely contested, but Mark Hudson opened the scoring on the half-hour, heading a Noone cross past former England international Paul Robinson. With Noone again the architect, Craig Bellamy had the chance to extend the lead before half-time, latching on to a through ball and thundering an effort against the crossbar. The home side left the field to a chorus of boos at the break and seemed revitalised at the start of the second half, promptly equalising. Substitute Colin Kazim-Richards held off the challenge of Ben Turner and fed Joshua King who slotted his chance between the legs of David Marshall. Within five minutes, Cardiff had regained the lead after a neat exchange between Heidur Helguson and Bellamy saw the Welsh international fire across goal to score from six yards. Blackburn had a great chance to level when Dickson Etuhu's deflected shot was parried by Marshall and a goalmouth scramble ensued, from which Mauro Formica clipped the bar when presented with an open goal. Mere minutes after coming off the bench, Joe Mason raced through on goal to net a third before Kim Bo-Kyung added a late fourth, his first for Cardiff, from the edge of the area to seal an emphatic win. Comfortably their finest away performance of the season, they dominated possession, set a high tempo and benefited from the savvy of Helguson, who had a hand in three of their goals.

Ahead of the visit of rock-bottom **Peterborough**, Cardiff were pleased to announce that Ben Turner was the latest key player to agree a new deal with the club. The Birmingham-born, 24-year-old man-mountain joined from Coventry City in August 2011 for a fee of £750,000. Still injured from a serious knee injury that had threatened his career, Mackay took a risk and it has proved to be a very astute piece of business. "Ben was someone I was desperate to sign from the moment I came to this club," Mackay confirmed. "I was delighted when that happened and then even more so based on the fantastic season he had for us last season." Turner started 42 games and scored a memorable late equaliser in the Carling Cup final against Liverpool, to take the tie to penalties. This season he has been just as impressive and integral. On extending his stay until 2016, Turner stressed: "This is the club I want to play for. The attitude at this club is spot on. We're trying to go forward as one. Everybody is working very hard together to make that happen. I've enjoyed every moment from day one. I want to play at the next level now and feel I can develop into that player at this club."

Cardiff played Peterborough in front of a bumper crowd in excess of 26,000, by far their biggest of the season against a side that they have struggled against in recent years. In October 2011, Cardiff lost 4–3 at London Road, despite leading 3–2 with three minutes remaining. Worse than that, in December 2009, they drew 4–4 after leading 4–0 at half-time. In the lead-up to this game, Malky Mackay told his players to forget the league table, in an attempt to avoid complacency setting in. Anyone watching this game would have thought that Peterborough were the form team and Cardiff rooted to the bottom. Mark Hudson's suspension saw Kevin McNaughton return to the side for his first start in a month, with Matthew Connolly stationed alongside Ben Turner. Hudson had been instrumental in Cardiff conceding only four goals in their last six games and his absence was to be keenly felt. Lining up in a 3–4–2–1 formation that seemed to cause Cardiff no end of problems, City also looked hesitant and devoid of creativity. They had the ball in the back of the net early on, when Heidar Helguson headed in a

Craig Bellamy free kick, but it was ruled out by the officials. Turner was then required to make an acrobatic overhead clearance from under his own crossbar to keep the game scoreless. The officials were to play a significant role in the opening goal on 22 minutes. Helguson was punished for a challenge on Gabriel Zakuani, but it looked like the decision – which Mackay would later describe as "incredible" – should have been awarded in Cardiff's favour as Zakuani had made contact first. To compound the sense of injustice, Michael Bostwick smashed the free kick past David Marshall, as the Cardiff manager raged on the touchline.

The same two players were soon involved in an incident at the other end, when a Helguson header was cleared by a last-ditch Zakuani challenge, as The Posh held on for a half-time lead. Just 70 seconds after the restart, Lee Tomlin fed Dwight Gayle who took a touch before firing past Marshall from 15 yards out. Rudy Gestede scored with a minute of the game remaining, converting from a Turner flick, but despite six minutes of injury time, Cardiff could not find an equaliser. Cardiff may have produced 20 attempts on goal, but they were lacklustre and the margin of victory could have been greater had it not been for some fine goalkeeping from Marshall. Mackay played down the defeat, claiming: "We were bound to lose at home at some point," but the standard of the performance that ended their proud unbeaten record will have been particularly disappointing.

Cardiff's last fixture before Christmas was a trip to the King Power Stadium to face fellow big-spenders **Leicester City**. Jordon Mutch and Kim Bo-Kyung returned to the side against a Foxes team looking to cement a place in the top six. Leicester peppered David Marshall's goal from the off. Dave Nugent broke down the right and his effort on goal required a strong hand from the Scottish international. From the resulting corner, he made a brilliant reaction stop to keep out a Wes Morgan header, before Andy King's curling effort struck a post. He also dealt with a couple of swerving Anthony Knockaert drives, before Cardiff scored from their first attack of the game. Mutch's cushioned header saw Craig Conway set off down the Leicester right, he pulled the ball back for Craig Bellamy who found the corner of the net with a powerful right-foot volley. He soon fired a similar chance over Kasper Schmeichel's bar, but the home side continued to press as King shot inches wide of the post and Jamie Vardy glanced a header against the bar. Cardiff brought on Rudy Gestede and Don Cowie early in the second half, in place of Helguson and Kim. Their introduction saw City improve and Gestede was unlucky not to score when his header deflected over the bar. Conway headed a Nugent effort off the line and substitute Aron Gunnarsson fluffed his lines when presented with a great chance late on. Cardiff rode their luck and held on to record an impressive victory in an end-to-end game, played at a ferocious tempo.

Third-placed **Crystal Palace** travelled to Cardiff on Boxing Day having lost only one of their previous 20 games. Former Cardiff favourite Danny Gabbidon lined up for the visitors, making his first start in almost a year. Craig Noone replaced Kim Bo-Kyung and Kevin McNaughton was drafted in for the absent Matthew Connolly and was tasked with keeping tabs on Palace's crown jewel Wilfried Zaha. The Eagles stunned the capacity crowd with an early goal, when captain Mile Jedinak headed in Owen Garvan's fourth-minute corner. They nearly added a second when Zaha cut inside and thumped his effort against the bar, with David Marshall tipping over Yannick Bolasie's follow-up. But McNaughton managed to restrict Zaha's influence and Cardiff were eventually able to take control of the contest. A minute before the break, Craig Bellamy motored down the Palace left and found Noone who rifled in the leveller. Bellamy's influence on the game increased as the second half progressed, testing Julián Speroni before efforts on goal from Peter Whittingham and Aron Gunnarsson. Ian Holloway felt his side should have had a penalty when Zaha and Rudy Gestede collided in the area, but Mackay instead felt that Zaha's theatrics warranted a second yellow card. A Bellamy corner resulted in the winning goal, as Gunnarsson headed in off the underside of the bar after 73 minutes. It was his sixth goal of the season, exceeding his tally for his first season with the club, with half of the season still remaining. A free transfer when his Coventry contract expired in 2011, Gunnarsson has been an influential figure in the heart of the City midfield, starting 48 games in the previous campaign. He is also the captain of the Icelandic national side, an honour bestowed on him at just 23.

A Whittingham free kick also skimmed the Palace bar as Cardiff ran out deserved winners and extended their lead at the top to five points. McNaughton, who had been in and out of the side in recent weeks but impressed against Palace, admitted after the game that he was suffering due to a lack of match practice. "I woke up the morning after we played Palace and felt like I had been hit by a bus. I felt the effects, but I've recovered now and am ready if needed." A veteran of several failed promotion campaigns, he also revealed that there is more steel and determination in the current squad, compared to previous years. "The gaffer has brought the right type of player to this club. The work ethic is different class. The players, each and every one of them gives his all in training sessions. It hasn't been like that all the time since I have been here, but there is no doubt the whole squad is up for it big time this season."

"Super Kev" retained his place in the starting line-up for the visit of **Millwall**. Aron Gunnarsson returned to the side and Rudy Gestede made his first start of the season up front. Despite regularly emerging from the bench, the tall, 24-year-old former French youth international has had to bide his time to force his way in to the side. Signed by Mackay in July 2011 after his Metz contract had expired, Gestede has shown plenty of raw promise, but a series of niggling injuries hampered his progress. He missed the first two months of the season but has been available since October and wasted no time in making a positive impression against The Lions.

Peter Whittingham, making his 250th appearance for the club, found Craig Noone on the wing, his jinking run ended in his cross finding Gestede, who flicked past former Cardiff keeper

David Forde to open the scoring. Millwall had a few opportunities to level, but David Marshall was equal to a couple of Darius Henderson efforts. Craig Bellamy lofted an effort narrowly over the bar and was the game's outstanding performer. Playing his third game in the space of seven days, his hunger and work ethic continues to be infectious. When those around him show signs of fatigue, he lifts the side by demonstrating his own exacting high standards. Whether tracking back to retain possession or breaking forward to counter-attack, he has the energy of a player half his age and his commitment to getting his hometown club promoted was evident for all to see. Despite a few knocks earlier in the season and a relative lack of goals, his knees are holding up and he appears to be fully focused on football, after struggling with well-documented personal issues.

Jordon Mutch replaced Aron Gunnarsson at half-time to reinforce the midfield and James Henry wasted a good chance before testing Marshall from a free kick, while Forde was equal to Noone's curled effort. But there were few second-half chances and Cardiff ground out another win to maintain a five-point lead at the Championship summit. The team topping the league at the end of the calendar year in each of

The customary pre-match huddle
© Jon Candy

Peter Whittingham converts from the spot in a 2–1 win against Leeds
© Jon Candy

Cardiff re-open the stadium after rebranding
© Jon Candy

Scarves for the new red home kit and blue away kit
© Bartosz Nowicki

Tommy Smith is frustrated by the Nottingham Forest defence
Image courtesy of akimages © 2013 Andrew Kearns

Craig Noone closely marshalled by Middlesbrough's André Bikey
© Jon Candy

Matthew Connolly heads the winner against Middlesbrough
© Jon Candy

David Marshall lofts the ball forward
© Mike Vaughan

Aron Gunnarsson heads the winner against Crystal Palace
© Jon Candy

A battered and bruised Ben Turner keeps a clean sheet against Ipswich
© Jon Candy

Fan favourite full back Kevin McNaughton
© Mike Vaughan

Craig Bellamy mounts an attack against Bristol City
© Sum of Marc

Matthew Connolly brings the ball out of defence
© Jon Candy

A Peter Whittingham set-piece delivery
© Sum of Marc

Cardiff kick off at Middlesbrough
© Bartosz Nowicki

January signing
Fraizer Campbell limbers up
© Jon Candy

On-loan Leon Barnett in action during a defeat at Peterborough
© Jon Candy

Veteran Icelandic international striker Heidur Helguson
© Jon Candy

Malky Mackay observing proceedings at Peterborough
© Jon Candy

Captain Mark Hudson marshalls the Cardiff defence
© Jon Candy

Rudy Gestede in action against Blackburn Rovers
© Jon Candy

South Korean international Kim Bo-Kyung in action
© Jon Candy

Owner Vincent Tan on a lap of honour after clinching promotion
© Jon Candy

Kim Bo-Kyung fires narrowly wide against Bolton
© Mike Vaughan

Craig Bellamy lines up a free kick
© Mike Vaughan

Kim Bo-Kyung maintains possession against Bolton
© Mike Vaughan

David Marshall celebrates after the trophy presentation
© Bartosz Nowicki

A premature pitch invasion at Hull on the final day of the season
© Bartosz Nowicki

The three Craigs at the parade: Bellamy, Conway and Noone
© Jon Candy

Aron Gunnarsson takes charge of the Championship trophy
© Bartosz Nowicki

The Cardiff City victory parade
© Gareth Thomas

The Millennium Centre lit up in blue at the Cardiff Bay festivities
© Lee Smith

the previous seven seasons had been promoted, so the Bluebirds certainly had history on their side. They had also demonstrated the requisite strength in depth to cope with injuries and the rigours of regularly playing twice a week. After a successful 2012, the hope was that Malky Mackay and his players could maintain their challenge in 2013.

# A lead extended in 2013

CARDIFF CRASHED OUT of the cup in January, but continued to rack up the points on the road.

1st January – Birmingham City (a)
5th January – Macclesfield Town (a)
12th January – Ipswich Town (h)
19th January – Blackpool (a)

With the January transfer window now open, attention turned to whether Cardiff would further reinforce their squad. The news that Peter Whittingham had injured his knee in the win against Millwall might have made Malky Mackay more inclined to survey the available options. Having created 30 chances for his team-mates and provided eight assists, his creative input would not be easy to replace in the interim. The knock was expected to rule him out for up to a month and left David Marshall as the only remaining ever-present in the Cardiff squad. There were five changes for the first game of 2013, with Matthew Connolly, Kim Bo-Kyung, Jordon Mutch, Joe Mason and Simon Lappin all drafted in for the trip to face **Birmingham City** at St Andrews. Lappin was a late inclusion due to Andrew Taylor being taken ill ahead of the match and Bellamy was selected for his fourth game in ten days. More than 2,200 Cardiff fans made the trip and were rewarded with a performance full of grit and determination, but short on chances and quality. Wade Elliott fired wide and Nathan Redmond forced a good save from Marshall early on, while Cardiff had only one attempt on goal in the first half. Fortunately, it led to the only goal of the game. Craig Conway cut inside on his left foot and forced a fine one-handed save from Jack Butland. Unable to steer the effort away from danger, he instead pushed it back in to play and Mason was the first to react to bag his fifth goal of the season.

A regular from the bench, but making only his eighth start, Mason was the revelation of Mackay's first season in charge. A £250,000 signing from Plymouth in July 2011, he was signed for the future but ended up starting 29 games in all competitions and emerging from the bench a further 16 times. He recorded eleven goals, three assists, opened the scoring in the Carling Cup final and received Cardiff's Young Player of the Year award. With a natural football intellect and great positional awareness, he can provide a link between midfield and attack, play up front or out wide. A wealth of options has seen him play less this year, but Mackay has admitted that he played too much in his first season and he remains an important member of the squad. Cardiff were almost two goals to the good early in the second half, when a Connolly shot was cleared off the line by Curtis Davies. Bellamy again provided an effervescent display while Mark Hudson and Ben Turner were rock solid at the back. City recorded their tenth clean sheet of the season, a ninth win in eleven games, opening up a nine-point gap between third-placed Crystal Palace.

Cardiff capped another fine display by revealing that Ben Nugent had signed a new deal until 2016, after his brisk ascent from the academy. "He is a kid with a fantastic attitude, great base and starting point," Mackay proudly announced. "He desperately wants to do well and learn. He has worked very hard for six months when he came up to seniors. He had injury problems in youth, so to come up and impress all the coaches and myself in such a short space of time shows the amount of work he has put in. We've rewarded him with a longer-term contract, he stood the test of going into the first team as a youngster, when you don't know if they will sink or swim or what is going to happen. Until they cross the line and play their first professional game at that level you can't be certain. Took that in his stride, captained the reserves and if he keeps working he is going to be a good player in the future. He has a lot of the right attributes to have a good career."

Nugent was one of the few senior players selected for a third round FA Cup tie at **Macclesfield Town**, as the majority of the squad were rested to protect against injury and fatigue. The decision proved to be a controversial one, as Mackay was accused of devaluing the competition, but he denied these claims and was prepared to justify his selection. "Our senior players played four games in eleven days and need a break," he reasoned. "I have the greatest respect for the FA Cup and remember clearly how excited I was the day I played my first tie in the English system. But we have certain guys who would run a high risk of injury if they play again this quickly. I am the one who knows where my players are, what level they are at and what chance there is of them breaking down with injuries. I am the only person who sees them every day. Those factors will have a huge bearing on my team selection." Stephen McPhail captained the side, making his first appearance since the Capital One Cup defeat at Northampton Town. Kadeem Harris made his debut, almost a year after signing for the club from Wycombe Wanderers, while Joe Ralls, Filip Kiss and Etien Velinkonja were also given the nod.

The gamble looked to have paid off when Cardiff opened the scoring after 57 minutes of an evenly matched contest. Young left back Declan John raced on to a Ralls pass to deliver an inviting cross which Nat Jarvis, who had recently returned from a loan spell at Forest Green Rovers, turned in from close range. Velinkonja could have added a second, but volleyed wide from an acute angle. With five minutes left, Jack Mackreth's far-post cross was bundled in by Matthew Barnes-Homer to equalise and three minutes later he added a deserved winner. Jarvis was penalised for shirt pulling in the area and Barnes-Homer confidently converted the resulting penalty, as the Silkmen progressed to the fourth round for the first time in their 138-year history. Cardiff's defeat against opponents 81 places below them in the Football League was portrayed as the weekend's giant killing and Mackay's decision was again questioned. But, like the defeat at Northampton, it was quickly forgotten and attention returned to sustaining their lead at the Championship summit.

Their options were boosted by the return of Tommy Smith, who had been out since damaging his hamstring at Watford in October. He had played eight games before his injury, Mackay claiming that his return was akin to a new arrival, describing him as somebody with a wealth of experience of the division and how to get promoted. "He has guile, is a quality footballer and can score a goal as well. Having Tommy available as we go into our 20 remaining league fixtures is like a new signing."

A week off did not appear to have a galvanising effect, as Cardiff subsequently laboured to a goalless draw with **Ipswich Town**, a very different proposition to the side they defeated at Portman Road. Mick McCarthy had since replaced Paul Jewell and overseen seven wins in 13 games to drag the Tractor Boys clear of the relegation places. Peter Whittingham's prompt return to the side was an unexpected bonus and Rudy Gestede led the attack, as all the usual suspects returned. A bitterly cold afternoon that featured both heavy rain and sleet, neither goalkeeper had a great deal to do as chances at either end were at a premium. Guirane N'Daw, the game's dominant force, struck Cardiff's post from 30 yards and

David Marshall comfortably dealt with a Frank Nouble effort. Bradley Orr almost diverted an Aron Gunnarsson cross in to his own net, until goalkeeper Scott Loach's intervention. Carlos Edwards had a shot deflected over the bar and David McGoldrick poked an effort wide of the post. The arrival of Tommy Smith in the second half failed to inspire Cardiff and they had the chance to win the game with a late Gunnarsson header but a draw was a fair result. Ahead of this match, Malky Mackay claimed that Cardiff needed ten more wins from their remaining 20 games to secure automatic promotion. They may have fallen short of winning three points on this occasion, but a point kept them ten points clear of third-placed Leicester.

In the days that followed, Mackay was keen to accentuate the positives and praise his miserly defence. After shipping so many goals at Bristol City, Charlton and Nottingham Forest, Cardiff had recorded eleven clean sheets in total and four in their last four games. He claimed that the dramatic improvement was due to working on the fundamentals of defending as a team in training.

"It's been about getting the basics right," he explained. "Getting the shape and a lot of repetition in what we have been doing. We needed to instil certain values into the players and the most important of those has been the work-rate and the ability to work for each other. People talk about the back four or the back five with David Marshall, but defending is the responsibility of the entire team. We attack as one unit and we defend as one unit."

A tough televised clash with **Blackpool** at Bloomfield Road was fast approaching, but with a two-week break to follow, the players could at least look forward to a week of warm weather training in Dubai – the perfect antidote to a freezing evening spent grafting on Blackpool's notoriously poor pitch.

Cardiff were without Craig Bellamy, ruled out with a virus, plus Ben Turner, a precautionary measure due to a tight hamstring. Kevin McNaughton was drafted in and Tommy Smith was paired with Joe Mason in attack against the manager-less Tangerines. Caretaker boss Steve Thompson almost witnessed his side take an early lead, when Tom Ince was put clean through on goal, but David Marshall managed to smother his effort. Both sides had early penalty appeals turned down, Joe Mason went down under a challenge from Kirk Broadfoot and Gary Taylor-Fletcher struck Andre Taylor's elbow, but they were waved away by the referee. Kim Bo-Kyung dragged a shot wide and Smith forced a save from Matthew Gilks as half-time approached. Mark Hudson failed to shake off an injury sustained in the first half and despite returning for the second period, he was soon replaced by Ben Nugent. A few minutes later, the league leaders went ahead when Aron Gunnarsson struck a post and Kim converted the rebound. Six minutes later, a lapse of concentration in the Cardiff defence saw Blackpool level. Tiago Gomes lofted a cross in to the area and Taylor-Fletcher rose above Taylor at the back post to head past Marshall. The goal gave Blackpool a lift but the Bluebirds soon re-established an advantage. On 64 minutes, Taylor broke down the left and his cross was only partially cleared, Smith volleyed towards goal and a deflection off Craig Cathcart's head deceived Gilks. Cardiff headed to the United Arab Emirates in fine fettle and were to be joined by their latest new recruit.

On 21st January, Cardiff signed Sunderland striker Fraizer Campbell for £650,000. The reasonable asking price was due to Campbell entering the final few months of his contract and also because of his recent injury history. He damaged his anterior cruciate knee ligaments in August 2010 and suffered a recurrence in April 2011. Despite scoring on his return in January

2012, he remained on the periphery of the Sunderland squad, but still managed to win his first England cap during this period. A Manchester United academy graduate, he spent time on loan at Royal Antwerp, Hull City and Spurs before joining Sunderland. At Hull, he scored 15 goals in 34 appearances during their 2007/08 promotion from the Championship and the hope was that he could aid a similar achievement at Cardiff.

"I'm delighted that this move has come off," Campbell revealed at his unveiling. "I've not played much football this season, so to get a fresh start at such an ambitious club as Cardiff is great for me. I can't wait to get back doing what I love here. Last time I was in the Championship we got promoted with Hull. That was brilliant and it's something I now want to do with Cardiff. I'm looking forward to the Leeds fixture now, that's next on my agenda. Hopefully I'll get to know the club and the lads a little bit better in the next week or so and then put my hand up to be involved at the start of February."

Simon Lappin also returned to the club, after a couple of loan appearances earlier in the season. Released by Norwich after a six-year association, he agreed an 18-month contract with Cardiff.

Cardiff's latest purchases preceded the release of their 2011/12 accounts, which highlighted the urgent need to secure promotion to the Premier League promised land. The club recorded losses of £13,605,000, increasing their overall debt to more than £83m. Cardiff City Football Club (Holdings) Limited, the umbrella company that incorporates the football club, owes £51,920,000 to creditors in the next twelve months and £31,175,000 to creditors in the future – £37,431,000 of the larger sum is owed to Vincent Tan, so not considered a pressing concern. The wage bill also increased from £13.9m-a-year to £18.5m, a figure that did not take in to account the club's summer spending spree. Turnover significantly increased, from £15,947,000 to £20,216,000, boosted by £2.3m for reaching the Carling Cup final. But there was also a rise in interest and administrative costs, plus £1.6m to pay off Dave Jones and release Malky Mackay from Watford. The Langston debt stood at £19,259,000, due to be repaid in 2016, with a one-off payment of £5m if Cardiff were to secure promotion. The club were clearly a long way from becoming sustainable, so promotion was essential. Failure to do so could have grave financial consequences.

# A new arrival flourishes

A FORMER ENGLAND international found his groove in February, as a controversial giveaway caused unrest.

2nd February – Leeds United (a)
9th February – Huddersfield Town (a)
16th February – Bristol City (h)
19th February – Brighton and Hove Albion (h)
24th February – Wolves (a)

Due to a lack of match practice, Fraizer Campbell was selected among the substitutes for the trip to **Leeds United**'s Elland Road, but he was to emerge from the bench and cap a memorable debut. Craig Bellamy returned after a stomach bug and Mark Hudson had recovered from the knock that saw him withdraw from the Blackpool game. The game came to life in the 23rd minute when Aron Gunnarsson was penalised for a back pass and Leeds were awarded a free kick twelve yards from goal. Several Cardiff players furiously opposed the decision, resulting in both Bellamy and David Marshall receiving bookings. The free kick was deflected wide, but Marshall's services were required ten minutes later. An El-Hadji Diouf free kick was helped on by Ross McCormack to Ross Barkley and with the goal at his mercy, Marshall somehow scrambled across to block the effort. Bellamy soon netted from a Kim Bo-Kyung flick, but it was ruled out for offside. Kim was withdrawn on the hour in favour of Campbell and with only his third touch, he opened the scoring. A poor clearance by Sam Byram was pounced upon by Bellamy and his shot was gladly diverted past Kenny by Campbell. Marshall made another fine save to keep out a Byram header from point-blank range, but once they took the lead, Cardiff never looked like relinquishing their advantage. Leeds manager Neil Warnock claimed that the result was "cruel" but also praised Cardiff's ability to "win ugly".

"I scored on my debut, who can ask for more than that?" a delighted Fraizer Campbell asked after the game, while Malky Mackay praised his match-winning front man's instant impact. "Fraizer is a man who is extremely humble. He has come in and quickly become part of the group. Fraizer must get up to speed because he hasn't played a lot of football recently, he must adapt to the frantic nature of Championship football and the work you have to put in. We knew he had a certain playing time in him at Leeds and not much more than we gave him. He is a willing runner, an intelligent footballer who knows how to score goals. He is a goal sniffer who has the proactive nature of a centre forward, as he showed. We are giving him the chance to prove again how good he can be and he wants it badly. He is grabbing this chance with two hands." Mackay also shed light on Cardiff's current approach to a congested fixture list, which included debuting a mantra coined to describe their pursuit of promotion. "We prepare in the same meticulous way for every match, home and away. This is now all about monotonous consistency and not being complacent. We have been consistent of late and have to maintain that momentum."

Cardiff returned to Yorkshire a week later to face **Huddersfield Town**, who were five games unbeaten at home, despite their lowly Championship status. Kevin McNaughton replaced the absent Ben Turner, with Matthew Connolly moved inside to cover at centre back. James Vaughan made a bright start, heading the first real attempt on goal wide after 17 minutes. He had the ball in the back of the Cardiff net soon after, but was penalised for obstructing David Marshall in the build-up. As half-time approached, Craig Bellamy thundered a free kick from 25 yards which Alex Smithies did well to turn around the post. In added time, Connolly also crashed a left-footed volley against the bar. McNaughton was withdrawn at the break due to a head wound, replaced by Ben Nugent, while Heidur Helguson was introduced in place of Kim Bo-Kyung. Neither change made a great deal of difference, Cardiff remained resolute in defence and short of ideas up front. Bellamy fired a chance wide and Craig Conway tested Smithies, but Huddersfield defended deep and were content with a point, as the game ended goalless. The home side left the field to a standing ovation, while Cardiff were left frustrated, but still managed to extend their lead with both Leicester and Hull losing. Unbeaten in eight games, having earned 20 points out of a possible 24, Mackay was justified in regarding the result as "a point gained".

They returned to South Wales to face **Bristol City**, looking to avenge a heavy defeat earlier in the campaign. Ben Nugent remained in situ and Fraizer Campbell made his first start, almost exactly a year since earning his sole England cap, in a friendly against Holland. Craig Noone tested Tom Heaton early on and a Craig Bellamy free kick required a stunning save to touch it over the bar. Nugent also put a decent chance over as Cardiff dominated proceedings, playing with a confidence and swagger that had been missing in recent weeks, despite their impressive results. They finally broke Bristol's resistance on the stroke of half-time. Campbell combined with Tommy Smith just inside the area, drawing Heaton out of his goal as Campbell lifted it over him with the outside of his right foot, high in to the net for a well-deserved half-time lead. It was a goal of Premier League class and City continued in the same vein after the break. Denied a penalty when Liam Fontaine looked to have a hold of Campbell's shirt, he soon added his and Cardiff's second. An Aron Gunnarsson long throw caused panic, as the man-of-the-moment adjusted his feet and swept the ball in from close range. Replaced by Heidur Helguson after 72 minutes, he received a rapturous response from the Cardiff faithful as they looked on track for a comfortable win. A late mix-up in the home defence resulted in Nugent heading past a stranded Marshall into his own net to give Bristol hope, but the win was secured. Cardiff had accrued 40 points at home, matching their haul from the previous season with eight more opponents still to entertain. They had also built an eight-point lead over second-placed Hull and eleven ahead of Watford in third, with a game in hand over both.

In advance of the midweek clash with **Brighton**, it was announced that every fan attending the game would be given a free red scarf, a gesture of goodwill from owner Vincent Tan. "We will be giving every Cardiff City supporter a free high-quality scarf as a means to keep warm," an email to fans declared. It was also stated that the motivation behind the giveaway was a way of "saying a big thank you for your support this season". The idea may have been well intended, but it instead served to shed light on the divide that remained with regards to the rebrand. The fact that the scarf in question was exclusively red, omitted 'City' and included the motto 'Fire & Passion' instilled a sense of paranoia in fans, who were already sceptical about how infrequently the team lined up in blue, with the black third kit usually favoured. There was also the added incentive of the chance to win a season ticket if you were photographed wearing the scarf. Some questioned whether the bluebird would become red in future, while others pondered if a change of name was next on the agenda.

Opposition to the changes had been largely

dormant due to such impressive league form, but the floodgates had been reopened and Mackay felt the need to publicly defend the scheme. "People still feel blue because that is in their hearts. I totally appreciate that," he said of the backlash, which was in danger of becoming an unwanted distraction. "They've had that for 50 years some of them and tradition is a big part of any football club. But we are going forward and that is the important part. Vincent has been nothing short of exceptional when it comes to the backing of this club. He's not only a very wealthy man, but, in terms of business, he's a very successful man. That being the case, his thoughts on the club moving forward were that he wanted to change colour. In return for that he would do certain things for the club and that is the trade-off. Despite people's belief in traditions, in the main they have accepted it. He's handing out the scarves because he wants people to get behind the team and that's it. It's his way of thanking fans for the amount of times they have turned out this year." With incessant speculation regarding potential protests and fans rejecting the scarf, all 25,000 were claimed and the overwhelming majority of the crowd sported their freebie throughout the game.

It would be easy to blame the hype

surrounding the game for City's subsequent defeat, but the truth of the matter is that Gus Poyet's side are a match for anyone on their day and also won in Cardiff during the previous campaign. Hard-working and comfortable in possession, Brighton are a team of few stand-out performers but operate as an effective unit. The impressive Liam Bridcutt dominated the game from the base of midfield and former Manchester United goalkeeper Tomasz Kuszczak is one the best in the division. Ben Turner was recalled after recovering from a foot problem and Cardiff picked up where they left off against Bristol City, creating openings from the off. After three minutes, Craig Bellamy found Fraizer Campbell who clipped the top of the Brighton bar, but the visitors were not to be breached. Kuszczak's crossbar was leading a charmed life, as he pushed a Bellamy effort on to the woodwork, but David Marshall was soon at full stretch to keep out a Leonardo Ulloa strike. An under-hit Dean Hammond back pass almost resulted in Bellamy rounding the keeper after 30 minutes, but Kuszczak managed to block his route to goal.

Despite concerted pressure, Brighton did not buckle and got their reward as half-time approached. David Lopez broke down the Cardiff right before delivering a cross which Andrea

Orlandi flicked past Marshall from close range. The Bluebirds were trailing for the first time since Boxing Day against a side that had not lost a game all season in which they had scored first. Craig Conway, on for Craig Noone in the second half, let fly from distance and Campbell had a header well saved, but the Seagulls were unflustered and sealed the win in the final minute. Again Lopez was the architect, sweeping forward and providing an assist for Ulloa to notch Brighton's second with the aid of a deflection, cutting Cardiff's lead to five points in the process.

With a game in hand, Mackay called for fans to remain calm after their first defeat in ten games. "Had we not played well and been beaten then I suppose I would be annoyed, but I thought we played well to create so many chances against a good team. We showed the spirit, determination and bravery the boys have got. We respect Brighton, they are a good team. But I thought we were excellent in making sure they did not keep the ball. We pressed them and had four or five good chances in the first half."

Despite occupying the final relegation spot, **Wolves** looked a tough opponent, as Cardiff sought a return to winning ways and to commence another of their unbeaten runs. They faced the prospect of kicking off at Molineux on

Sunday with only a two-point cushion at the top, but Hull's 4–1 thrashing at Bolton the day before ensured that Cardiff's lead remained intact. Don Cowie and Craig Conway were selected in place of Craig Noone and Tommy Smith as Cardiff took the early initiative. Peter Whittingham saw his drive whistle just over Carl Ikeme's bar after 17 minutes and three minutes later they hit the front. An Aron Gunnarsson long throw was flicked on and Fraizer Campbell rose above a cluster of Wolves defenders to head in from four yards. Cardiff's passing and movement was streets ahead of a nervous, tentative Wanderers side. Cowie headed narrowly wide before his shot was spilled by Ikeme, but Bellamy's follow-up was cancelled out by an official's flag. The introduction of Kevin Doyle and Sylvan Ebanks-Blake gave Dean Saunders' side more cutting edge in the second period, as Doyle went close on a couple of occasions, but Cardiff and Campbell were soon to score again. An in-swinging Bellamy free kick found the unmarked striker, to head in his fifth goal in five games and give his side an insurmountable lead. Bakary Sako did his best to drag Wolves back into the contest. His free kick deflected off the Cardiff wall and wrong-footed David Marshall with 20 minutes remaining, but it proved to be a consolation goal, despite laying on a golden chance for Ebanks-Blake late on, which he fluffed.

Mackay hailed Cardiff's fine performance, claiming: "It was the best we've played this season in parts. In the first half we were excellent." He also praised the travelling support, which totalled 2,500, adding: "It was great to see the Cardiff fans come out in their droves and I want them to back us in every game from here on in." But in the days that followed, Mackay was required to jump to the defence of Peter Whittingham against claims that his influence had waned and that he would benefit from a break. His last goal was against Watford on 23rd October, 20 games ago, despite missing only one game since. Signed from Aston Villa in January 2007, only Kevin McNaughton and Stephen McPhail have been at the club longer. Whittingham had played close to 300 games for the club and was the reigning Football League Player of the Year. Transformed from a left winger to a central midfielder by former manager Dave Jones, he may score fewer goals but has a far greater influence on proceedings.

A firm fan favourite, some feel that Mackay stations him too deep and that his creative capabilities would be better utilised further forward. His manager is undoubtedly a big fan and had already rewarded him with three new contracts during his first season in charge.

"Peter is someone who over the whole of this season has been incredibly consistent for us," Mackay explained. "He's not a forward, he's a midfielder and if you get the bonus of some goals from a midfielder then that is great. I see the value of him. I see his maturity now. I see the difference in the boy now from the boy I spoke to the first day I took over at Cardiff. They are completely different people to be honest. There's a lot of sides to his game now compared to someone, who before maybe sat on the periphery of a team and when it got into his area he did something with it. Now he is in the middle of everything that goes on for the whole 90 minutes. Now he's even more of a team player than he ever was."

Vincent Tan was also required to defend his actions as February drew to a close. After his scarf giveaway had received an unexpected backlash from some quarters, there was further consternation when he was interviewed by BBC Wales. Tan alluded to further rebranding if the club reached the Premier League and responded to a question about a potential name-change by revealing: "We will think about it when we know the final result of this season." Changing the team's colours required no external consultation, but amending the name would require the approval of both the Welsh and English Football Associations. Should the club be promoted, they would also need the go-ahead from the Premier League and the application would need to be submitted by 1st April.

Tan promptly issued a statement to clarify the situation, which indicated that a new name was not on the agenda. "I can assure all supporters that we will not be changing our name from Cardiff City Football Club, a club I am very proud to be a part of. Our name is our identity and remains at our core. I would not want any of our supporters to be concerned that this change would be made, hoping that this personal commitment from myself removes any fears. I believe the colour change is positive and will bring good tidings to Cardiff City Football Club. At this point of time, no decision has been made to change the club crest for the next season. For the present day, all I would ask is that we all join together, continuing your excellent support at what is a critical juncture in our season. Our collective aim is to back Malky Mackay and his team as they work hard to bring us all success. Working together we can achieve great things in the name of Cardiff City Football Club."

Having returned from Israel, Robert Earnshaw

left to join Toronto FC on 28th February, for the start of the new MLS season. His second spell at the club may have proved to be a disappointment, but he remains a club legend and will always be treasured by Cardiff supporters.

# A spring wobble

CARDIFF FALTERED IN March, causing some to question whether City had the required stamina and mental strength to secure promotion, after so many near-misses in the recent past.

2nd March – Middlesbrough (a)
5th March – Derby County (h)
12th March – Leicester City (h)
16th March – Sheffield Wednesday (a)
30th March – Peterborough United (a)

March commenced with news that Dato Chan Tien Ghee had resigned as a director at the club in order to give his full attention to other business interests in Malaysia. Instrumental in the arrival of Vincent Tan, Chan was a popular figure and both the club and manager moved to praise his efforts. "We are greatly indebted to TG who since joining in 2010 has been instrumental in the progress of the club to where it is today," read a club statement. "We wish TG all the very best in his new undertakings." Malky Mackay added: "In the future, when people look back at this period, it will be clear that TG played a hugely important role for this football club. He had a massive commitment to Cardiff City and cares deeply about this club. He has put Cardiff City on the map in Malaysia. He is a good man and has done an awful lot for Cardiff City FC."

Cardiff suffered their first away defeat in ten games at **Middlesbrough**'s Riverside Stadium in their first spring encounter. Kevin McNaughton started in place of the absent Mark Hudson and they sorely missed their captain. On the back foot from the very start, Sammy Ameobi headed over Grant Leadbitter's free kick after just three minutes. The talented Newcastle youngster, who had signed on loan only days earlier, was then instrumental in the opening goal. His cross was converted by former England international Kieron Dyer from six yards out, his first goal since May 2007. Ameobi added a sumptuous second, beating two Cardiff players with close control on the edge of the penalty area before curling past a helpless David Marshall. Two down after 17 minutes, Cardiff were enjoying plenty of the ball without really threatening the Boro defence. Peter Whittingham had an attempt saved by Jason Steele, but that was as good as it got in the first half. Ben Nugent and Heidur Helguson were introduced after the interval, but it was Aron Gunnarsson who eventually gave City some hope. He headed in a Craig Bellamy corner from close range midway through the second half, but despite enjoying a territorial advantage, they created very few clear-cut chances. Fraizer Campbell wasted their best opportunity to snatch a point, heading Whittingham's cross wide with only seconds remaining. A rare off-day that saw their lead at the top again cut to five points.

With games coming thick and fast, Cardiff didn't have to wait long for an opportunity to get the Middlesbrough defeat out of their system. **Derby County** visited Cardiff City Stadium for a midweek clash a few days later, but Mackay's men were again off-colour. Any suggestion that the Rams would be a pushover, after six games without a win, was disproved very early in the encounter. Their performance was typified by their forwards, the aggressive, physical Chris Martin and the eager, industrious Conor Sammon. Craig Bellamy missed the game after rolling his ankle in training, replaced by Heidur Helguson, who paired up with Fraizer Campbell for the first time.

Paul Coutts saw a decent attempt on David

Marshall's goal repelled, but the visitors were soon aggrieved when two contentious decisions went against them. Cardiff lost possession, allowing Derby to break and Martin found the bottom corner of the City net, only for it to be ruled out for offside. They also had a penalty claim ignored by the referee, when Ben Turner dived in to block a Jeff Hendrick drive and the ball struck the defender's arm. Cardiff were fortunate to be on level terms at the break, but these scares failed to ignite their second-half performance. Coutts was again denied by Marshall, as the Cardiff crowd began to get restless.

Craig Noone was introduced to add more attacking intent, but his arrival coincided with Derby taking a deserved lead. A third defeat in four games looked a very real possibility when Cardiff again failed to retain the ball. Derby broke and found Sammon with time and space to convert from inside the area, with only 15 minutes remaining. Joe Mason and Rudy Gestede were brought on and, fortunately, Cardiff rallied and restored parity with eight minutes remaining. Andrew Taylor charged forward and whipped in an inviting cross for the diminutive Noone to head in at the far post. Gestede could have secured an undeserved win late on but volleyed over.

Mackay praised his side's "character and

resilience" post-match, but Cardiff were having a wobble at the worst possible time. Ben Turner, never a man to mix his words, provided a far sterner appraisal. "We haven't really had a period when we have struggled for results. This has been our worst block of four. Every time, after a defeat, we've bounced back with a win and that's credit to the players and staff here. This time, after a defeat at Middlesbrough, we've responded with a draw and that's not what we wanted. We weren't at our best on any level. It's hard to say why, but we didn't pass as well as we could and let our moves break down through sloppy passing." But he was also keen to stress that: "Every player is confident we have what it takes to finish the job."

Fortunately, none of their rivals looked equipped to capitalise and they retained a five-point lead, with a game in hand. An evident dip in form saw calls for Mackay to shuffle his pack and rotate his leggy side. Craig Noone, Kim Bo-Kyung and Joe Mason were the names nominated by fans and commentators for more first-team football, while criticism of Peter Whittingham continued to mount. Turner missed the subsequent game, another evening clash, against play-off contenders **Leicester City**. Ben Nugent kept his place and was partnered by Mark Hudson, returning from an ankle injury that had seen him miss the previous two games.

Chris Wood had the first chance of note after nine minutes, which was dealt with by David Marshall. Matthew Connolly also did well to block efforts from Lloyd Dyer and David Nugent in quick succession. Hudson required lengthy attention on his troublesome ankle, but managed to play on and made a great tackle on Wood when he threatened to break through the City defence. Cardiff created a few half-chances, but opted to introduce Craig Bellamy at the break in place of Craig Noone. Hudson was unable to return and Kevin McNaughton also replaced the Cardiff captain. Bellamy created an opening for Tommy Smith and Fraizer Campbell almost converted the resulting cross. When Wood finally pierced the Cardiff defence on the hour, Marshall stood tall and blocked his path to goal. As the game entered the final 20 minutes, Leicester took the lead. Michael Keane headed a Danny Drinkwater corner against the post and when Sean St Ledger returned the ball in to the Cardiff box, Keane buried his second chance.

Substitute Rudy Gestede squandered a great chance to equalise with six minutes left, heading over a Peter Whittingham cross, but he made amends in added time to salvage another point.

Mackay claimed: "Our equaliser was reward for the way we kept fighting to the end," but despite showing admirable spirit, only one win in five games was hardly championship-winning form. They also faced an injury crisis in the heart of their defence, with both Mark Hudson and Ben Turner struggling with ankle injuries. A trip to Sheffield Wednesday only days away and Mackay opted to recruit an emergency loan signing to tide them over.

Leon Barnett arrived on an initial month-long loan deal on 14th March and would go straight in to the starting line-up to face the Owls. The 27-year-old had made eight Premier League appearances for Norwich City during the season, but had not played since the end of January. Formerly of Luton Town and West Brom, Barnett joined Norwich in January 2011, after an initial spell on loan. Promoted from the Championship with both the Baggies and the Canaries, Mackay was delighted to be able to sign such a versatile, experienced player at such short notice. "Leon is an experienced defender and will add quality to our ranks over the coming weeks. He's quick, aggressive and a combative player, an excellent professional who has been involved in promotion pushes and is a good lad too. I've no doubt he'll fit in very well with the squad and I would like to thank Chris Hughton and Norwich City for their help in bringing Leon in, it's very much appreciated."

In the lead-up to the games, **Sheffield Wednesday** manager Dave Jones confirmed that he no longer had any fondness for his former club, explaining: "I have good memories, but I left that club and moved to another. It doesn't mean anything to me whatsoever. My professionalism kicks in. Full stop." He also praised his successor and revealed that he expected Mackay to finally lead Cardiff to the top flight. "Malky has done a good job there and I believe they will earn automatic promotion. It's a question of whether they go up as champions or runners-up."

Cardiff entered their final ten games of the season with a makeshift centre back pairing of debutant Barnett and Ben Nugent, who were sure to have their work cut out against a big, physical Wednesday team. Craig Bellamy, Heidur Helguson and Don Cowie were also drafted in against a side on the fringes of the relegation places. A scrappy affair, the main talking points from the first half revolved around refereeing decisions.

Owls keeper Chris Kirkland fumbled a Bellamy corner and was fortunate to be awarded a free kick after some pushing was spotted. Leroy Lita had a penalty appeal turned down and also escaped punishment when he appeared to catch Cowie in the face with an elbow. The Scottish midfielder was soon the centre of attention for an altogether different reason, when he opened the scoring in the dying moments of the half. Wednesday failed to clear a Bellamy corner and the ball fell to Cowie on the edge of the box, who saw his low shot elude everyone, including Kirkland, via the aid of a deflection.

One of Mackay's trusted lieutenants, Cowie has found first-team opportunities hard to come by this year, after an influx of midfielders in the summer. An influential figure at Watford, under Mackay, he followed his manager to Cardiff in July 2011 when his contract expired. He started 51 games in all competitions in his first season with the Bluebirds, impressing with his stamina and determination. A Scottish international, he remained a valued squad member, able to fill in right across the midfield.

The second half continued in the same vein, scrappy with few chances at either end. Matthew Connolly netted Cardiff's second after 65 minutes, heading an in-swinging Peter Whittingham free kick past a hesitant Kirkland who remained rooted to his line. Miguel Llera saw a free kick tipped over by David Marshall, from what was Wednesday's first real attempt on goal. Lita had a goal ruled out for offside late on, but City were good value for their tenth away win of the season. They received a further boost with news that Hull and Watford had also both lost, extending Cardiff's lead to seven points with a game in hand.

Having seen an eleven-point lead at the start of February dwindle to just four ahead of this game, questions were being asked as to whether the Bluebirds were on course for yet another late collapse. Instead, they were now able to enjoy a two-week break with a commanding advantage after recording another gritty win. The only dampener was news that Mark Hudson's ankle ligament injury would rule him out for the remainder of the season. One of Cardiff's star performers, his presence and leadership would be a big loss, but Leon Barnett performed well on his debut and was an able deputy. Jordon Mutch also declared himself fit for selection, having only played once in 2013 due to a nagging foot injury. As the transfer window for loan signings drew to a close, the club were inundated with requests for Joe Mason, but Mackay confirmed that he was very much in his plans and going nowhere. With half a dozen clubs having rung to ask about the player, Mackay reaffirmed that he was excited about Joe's future with Cardiff City and he was adamant that he was part of the first-team squad.

Suitably refreshed, Cardiff faced two games in three days over the Easter period, a trip to London Road to face **Peterborough** on the Saturday before hosting Blackburn on bank holiday Monday. Craig Bellamy was absent for the first of these games, but Ben Turner returned to partner Leon Barnett for the first time and Jordon Mutch was named among the substitutes. Dwight Gayle, a scorer in the reverse fixture, had the game's first chance, a shot from 18 yards that David Marshall did well to hold. Cardiff went close after 17 minutes when Peter Whittingham fired narrowly over the Posh goal from the edge of the area. Six minutes later, they had the lead when Heidur Helguson provided the assist for Aron Gunnarsson's eighth goal of the season.

Whittingham soon went close once again and Lee Tomlin had a couple of efforts on the Cardiff goal late in the half. Peterborough applied more pressure after the interval as Kane Ferdinand's header was well saved and Craig Alcock lofted a chance over the City crossbar. They eventually found a way back in to the game when Don Cowie lost possession and upended Mark Little in his own area. Grant McCann gratefully lashed in United's equaliser from the spot and only seven minutes later he found himself tasked with yet another penalty. Matthew Connolly fouled Gayle with only ten minutes remaining and McCann again deceived Marshall to give Peterborough a deserved lead. Rudy Gestede had a couple of late chances but Darren Ferguson's side held on to do the double over Cardiff, with a pair of 2–1 wins. Mackay was left to rue his side's defending and the award of the first penalty, but attention quickly turned to Blackburn Rovers.

# The promised land

D ESPITE A SUCCESSION of draws, April proved to be a month that Cardiff fans will never forget as promotion and the championship were secured in consecutive games, before the coronation in front of an adoring capacity crowd.

    1st April – Blackburn Rovers (h)
    6th April – Watford (a)
    9th April – Barnsley (h)
    13th April – Nottingham Forest (h)
    16th April – Charlton Athletic (h)
    20th April – Burnley (a)
    27th April – Bolton Wanderers (h)

Ahead of their game with **Blackburn**, Cardiff knew that by gaining 14 points from their final eight games, they would ensure promotion to the Premier League. They first had to navigate a Rovers side struggling at the wrong end of the table under a caretaker manager. Craig

Bellamy returned to the side and under-fire Peter Whittingham dropped to the bench for the first time in the league during Malky Mackay's reign. Jordon Mutch and Kim Bo-Kyung were also selected to freshen up the midfield. Mackay was rewarded for his bold team selection with an impressive display that reinvigorated his side's relatively patchy recent form. Blackburn goalkeeper Jake Kean saw his goal peppered with attempts, first from a rasping Bellamy free kick on seven minutes. A minute later he flapped at a corner and Fraizer Campbell wasted the opportunity to capitalise on his mistake. With almost half-an-hour played, Danny Murphy was lucky not to concede a penalty when he appeared to handle the ball in his area. Blackburn thought they had taken the lead ten minutes before half-time when Leon Best converted a chance created by Morten Gamst Pedersen, but he slightly mistimed his run and it was chalked off.

Campbell struck the bar before Bellamy and Mutch both went close, but eventually got the goal their efforts deserved five minutes before the break. Campbell found himself completely unmarked six yards out to nod in Bellamy's corner, his first goal in six games. Blackburn's prospects were dealt a further blow six minutes after the break when Kean was stretchered off, replaced in goal by debutant Grzegorz Sandomierski. He was soon required to make a smart save from the impressive Kim, but Pedersen almost caught out David Marshall with a free kick from distance that had him backtracking on 68 minutes. Sandomierski did well to deny Ben Turner from eight yards but six minutes from time, Cardiff finally sealed the win. Substitute Joe Mason jinked past two defenders before creating the space to drive low in to the Blackburn net. In added time, Mason was brought down by Scott Dann to allow fellow substitute Whittingham to extend the lead from the spot, his first goal in more than five months.

Delighted with the performance, Mackay showered praise on his re-energised Bluebirds, stating: "I thought our team was exceptional today. Anyone that came to the stadium to watch us saw a fantastic performance. We were playing against a very experienced team, their front six were incredibly experienced and we knew that if we didn't press them from the first minute we would allow them to show their qualities. We ended up with 18 shots on target in the first half before Fraizer got the goal, so I'm delighted to dominate the way we did, keep a clean sheet and eventually come out with the three goals."

A comprehensive victory was the ideal

preparation for a potentially pivotal encounter with third-placed **Watford** the following weekend. The Hornets would first face second-placed Hull, in a game that would benefit Cardiff with one or both of their closest rivals dropping points. Ahead of the televised Vicarage Road clash, Fraizer Campbell, who was a doubt for the game after departing the Blackburn game with a knock, revealed his delight at scoring regularly for his new club and his future international aspirations. "I would love to play for my country again," he stated, "If I can play on a regular basis for Cardiff and impress every week, there is always the chance of playing at international level. The important factor is that I must focus on playing for Cardiff City, enjoy my football and know that if I play well enough consistently then international rewards will come. My aim is to perform at the highest level possible. I have played Premier League football before, but my ambition now is to compete at that level for Cardiff City."

Watford's 1–0 win at Hull significantly improved their chances of remaining in the mix for automatic promotion; it also benefited Cardiff as it maintained the gap between first and second. With so much at stake for both sides, City's encounter with Gianfranco Zola's side, who were looking for their first home win in three games, was predictably tentative. Cardiff, resplendent in their blue kit for the first time since the end of November, made one change with Joe Mason replacing the injured Fraizer Campbell. But they were forced to make a further adjustment after ten minutes, when Matthew Connolly had to be replaced by Kevin McNaughton.

Kim Bo-Kyung soon forced a fine save from Manuel Almunia and Craig Conway's effort from the edge of the box flew just wide. Ben Turner headed narrowly over, before Troy Deeney blazed over from ten yards out at the other end. An over-zealous Aron Gunnarsson challenge on Cristian Battocchio ignited a heated exchange on the touchline between Mackay and Zola's assistant Giancarlo Corradini, but the Icelander escaped a caution. In the second half, Joe Mason capitalised on a Joel Ekstrand mistake and embarked on the Watford goal, but found Almunia his equal. Marshall soon upstaged his opposite number by somehow clawing away a Deeney header. Conway again went close, while substitute Fernando Forestieri only narrowly cleared the bar from distance and dragged another effort just wide. Kim had an attempt deflected wide and Deeney found himself crowded out in the Cardiff box late on. Both sides matched each other blow for blow, but the point certainly suited Cardiff more.

They could now look forward to three successive home games, starting with a midweek clash against **Barnsley**. They knew that if they kept their end of the bargain and results went their way, they could be promoted before playing their next away game. Mackay was full of praise for his side, who recorded another clean sheet and provided a very professional performance. "I'm very pleased with the intelligence of my team's performance. We came away from home and kept a clean sheet against the highest scorers in the league. They started with two strikers who have scored an awful lot of goals between them this year. We kept a clean sheet which was fantastic and it was our 16th of the season. We started really well. In the first half we passed it very well. In the second half they had to come at us and chase us. They were at home and they needed to win. It was a really dogged second half. I'm very proud of my group." Mackay also confirmed that Fraizer Campbell would miss the next couple of games with the shin injury he sustained against Blackburn.

Their next opponents Barnsley, fresh from eleven wins in their previous 18 matches, hovered one point above the relegation zone and were content to remain compact and soak up Cardiff's pressure. City selected Tommy Smith ahead of

Craig Conway and Kevin McNaughton started, with Matthew Connolly still sidelined. Bellamy was again at his effervescent best, driving his team forward and striking the woodwork, while Jordon Mutch went close with a couple of fierce efforts. But despite nine attempts on goal, they were unable to find a first-half breakthrough. Kim Bo-Kyung saw his drive deflect behind for a corner just before the hour and his corner resulted in the opening goal. His set-piece was delivered with pace and Ben Turner stuck out a leg to divert it past Luke Steele, recording his first goal of the season. Heidur Helguson replaced Joe Mason to provide a more physical presence up front and Peter Whittingham replaced Kim.

Barnsley introduced a trio of strikers as they sought some reward for their efforts, but Leon Barnett proved to be a formidable presence in the Cardiff defence. Helguson had two late chances to seal the victory, heading wide and shooting tamely when through on goal. It was to prove costly. In the seventh minute of injury time, Stephen Foster's tame shot took a cruel deflection and crept past David Marshall in to the empty net. It was the last action of the game and denied Cardiff the chance to seal promotion in their next game, against **Nottingham Forest**. They now required a maximum of seven points from their last seven games but, despite this setback, promotion was now looking inevitable.

Mackay confirmed that he had no qualms about the amount of injury time played, a contentious issue among the players and fans after only five minutes were signalled. He confirmed that the referee had informed him that the added time was for an injury sustained by Kevin McNaughton. Malky instead focused on the encouraging performance of Jordon Mutch, explaining: "I threw him in and asked him to perform, he's done that and more. Jordon has not played so much this season, but now he's played twice in quick succession. He has been excellent in both matches. The way he carries the ball and leaves people for dead with the ball under control is outstanding. It shows the potential the lad has. His foot injury has been an issue and it is something we will take a look at in the summer again, but he is ready to play and has done an excellent job."

In the days that followed, Craig Bellamy also granted a rare interview, revealing that promotion with Cardiff would be the highlight of his career. "The impact the Premier League could have on the community, youngsters and also businesses will be great. That would be my legacy. When you get to my age you realise that in a couple of years' time you don't know what will happen. Have I got another big injury in me? Probably not. I can have a sense of achievement in that while I didn't start my career here, I did end it here and I ended on the right note. I was able to give something back to the area I grew up in. If we do go up, of course that would be the highest achievement in my career. I wouldn't mind sitting here in a month's time having achieved that and telling people about it. It's difficult to say it at the moment because I have to show respect to Hull and Watford. I don't want them to turn around and say, 'Look at Cardiff, they think they are already up'. Because we aren't yet. But we are getting there. And if we do reach the Premier League, it will take us on to another level. The impact promotion could have on my community could last years and years. That is what drives me on. That is what gives me satisfaction at this football club. We could make an impact that no previous Cardiff City team has been able to."

Mackay received a boost ahead of the Forest game, negotiating an extension to Leon Barnett's loan deal which was due to expire after the game. He would now remain with the club until the end of the season. Barnett was named man-of-the-match against Barnsley and Cardiff had conceded only two goals in his five games thus far. He would have to be at his best against a resurgent Forest side, unbeaten in ten games under the returning Billy Davies and making a late charge towards the play-off places. Adlène Guedoiura, sent off in his side's 3–1 win back in October, was influential in the early stages and fired a shot into the side netting. Greg Halford's deliberate block on Kim Bo-Kyung earned him a yellow card and conceded a free kick in a dangerous position. Craig Bellamy's delivery found Heidur Helguson unmarked at the far post to head in his ninth goal of the season. Lewis McGugan thought he had levelled when he muscled Aron Gunnarsson off the ball and curled past David Marshall, but he was penalised for the challenge and the goal was ruled out. When Marshall parried a Henri Lansbury effort, he was fortunate that Darius Henderson mis-controlled and wasted the opportunity. With three minutes of the half remaining, Henderson lashed out at Gunnarsson as they jostled ahead of a Forest free kick. His arm caught the City midfielder in the face and the Forest forward received a red card. Bellamy clipped the post from a free kick, as Cardiff exploited their numerical advantage in the second half. Forest failed to clear and Rudy Gestede, a half-time replacement for the injured Helguson, rose highest to meet Andrew Taylor's cross and power a header past Karl Darlow.

Cardiff bagged a third headed goal when

Gestede met another Bellamy free kick, which glanced off the far post. Craig Noone saw a late attempt rebound off a post as the Bluebirds ruined Forest's unbeaten run. A record crowd of 25,588 left the ground knowing that a solitary point from their remaining four games would ensure promotion.

Next up were **Charlton Athletic**, the Championship's form team and conquerors of Cardiff in bizarre fashion earlier in the season. "That was certainly among our worst performances," Mackay claimed ahead of the game, revealing that November's 5–4 defeat proved to be something of a defining moment. "It was a turning point in our away form, certainly away we had a look at the way we were playing. We tweaked a couple of things in the way we played which has certainly helped. Right now we have one of the best away records in the league."

In a reflective mood, he also praised the Cardiff fans for their support throughout the campaign and during his reign as a whole. "I came to South Wales and took a new job with a new team and had new people around me. It has been a great experience and it will be something we really enjoy and are proud of. I realise winning helps whether a manager is taken to by supporters. Invariably over the last 18 months it's been positive. When I've needed them, they have been there. When we've been below par, or suffered disappointments like the play-off semi-final, they have been superb. I have felt at home down here, whether it's been the passion of the people in the street or the people within the club, there is a fantastic warmth I have felt. Those loyal fans were tested and asked to back the team through the colour change and I have great admiration for them. The amount of people who travel away is superb and I will be forever grateful for the backing we have had in the last two years."

On Tuesday, 16th April – 53 years to the day since Cardiff City were last promoted to the top flight – the 2013 vintage stood on the brink of repeating the feat. Craig Noone and Rudy Gestede started in place of Tommy Smith and the absent Heidur Helguson, for what proved to be a tense contest in front of an expectant full house. Addicks captain Johnnie Jackson almost spoiled the occasion with a clever first-half free kick. With everyone expecting a cross, he went for goal and his attempt struck David Marshall's post. Craig Bellamy, in the thick of the action at both ends, fired a shot over the bar, while Kim Bo-Kyung had the opportunity to provide him with a golden chance, but a heavy touch wasted it. Both sides continued to cancel each other out into the second half when Ben Hamer kept out a Leon Barnett deflected drive. Marshall was at full stretch to tip away Ricardo Fuller's effort and Craig Noone had a header ruled out for offside. With ten minutes remaining, news filtered through that Millwall had taken the lead against Watford and a cheer reverberated around the ground. With Hull also losing, even a defeat would suffice for Cardiff, but results could change and Cardiff were looking good value to secure a draw.

When the final whistle eventually blew at 0–0, Bellamy dropped to his knees as ecstatic fans invaded the pitch. Players and officials made a dash for the tunnel as the stands emptied and jubilant fans chanted "The Blues are going up". Announcer Ali Yassine's confirmation that "Cardiff City are in the Premier League" prompted joyous scenes, as the pitch filled with fans, chanting for the team to return for a lap of honour. When stewards managed to clear the area, players and staff, accompanied by their families, circled the pitch, revelling in the occasion. But the festivities were cut short when fans once again took to the pitch, as the singing and dancing continued.

Vincent Tan was also prominent in the festivities and he confirmed that there were no plans for further rebranding. "No more changes to the shirt and the name will stay the same, always," he stated. His focus was instead fixed on ensuring that Cardiff establish themselves in the top flight. "Malky Mackay has done a great job, he is a great manager. It is wonderful, a fantastic feeling. I looked at all the fans and everybody is so happy. I feel good and now we need to strategise how to stay up in the Premier League. That will be a tough one for us. But it is not an impossible challenge for us. God willing we would like to stay up there a long time."

He also revealed plans to provide Mackay with another substantial transfer kitty and expected him to provide value for money. "We need to strategise well and we would like to spend some money, maybe £20 to £25 million. Others have spent a big amount of money and don't do well, so we will try to spend smartly."

With a new TV deal with Sky and BT worth £3bn over the next three years, there has never been a more lucrative time to be in the top flight. Industry experts were also predicting that promotion could generate as many as 5,000 jobs and £120m for the area. There is also the small matter of the South Wales derby of course, which is sure to raise the profile of Welsh football on a global scale. It was also mission accomplished for an emotional Craig Bellamy, who helped his local team reach the top flight at the second attempt. "To have the people I truly love around me as well, to share that moment with me was special. To see my dad and my son was special. A one-off. For my dad to see Cardiff promoted to the Premier League and for his son to play a part in that makes it even more special for me. It hit home for me a little bit in that moment. It's been emotional. He told me 'I'll die a happy man'."

Cardiff next headed to Turf Moor to face a **Burnley** side looking to secure their Championship status. City were looking to clinch the title with two games to spare, but it remained to be seen whether they would be sufficiently motivated after already achieving their primary goal. Those fears were quickly banished as Mackay's men took control of the contest, utilising a five-man midfield with Craig Conway replacing Craig Bellamy. Rudy Gestede was the lone front man and had the first chance of the game, volleying just over from 25 yards. Kim Bo-Kyung laid off a Gestede knock down for Aron Gunnarsson to shoot narrowly wide and Conway saw a deflected effort well saved by Lee Grant. He went one better in the 27th minute, cutting in from the left and jinking past three defenders before finding the top corner of the Burnley net. The Scottish international continued to cause the home side problems and was chopped down by Kieran Trippier, earning the Clarets right back a yellow card, while Ross Wallace was lucky to escape at least a caution when his arm struck the impressive Kim in the face just before half-time.

Having failed to produce any notable attempts on goal in the first half, Burnley improved after the break. Sam Vokes and Martin Paterson both headed over David Marshall's bar before he produced a superb save to deny Danny Ings late on. In the final minute, he got a hand to David Edgar's header, but failed to keep it out as Burnley nicked a point. A point proved sufficient for Cardiff to claim the title, their first since winning Division Four in 1992/93.

For the second time in a week, players celebrated in front of the City supporters and, as is customary on such occasions, Mackay was also thrown in to the air as part of the festivities. When he finally returned to his feet, he eulogised his players and their achievements. "It's absolutely fantastic, I'm delighted for everyone at the football club. It was obviously a tremendous feeling on Tuesday night but for us to go and win the title is something that we then spoke about within a day. We wanted to go and get the boys their medal and win the Championship. We've been sitting there since late November and it's been an awful long time for us to be top and be chased and be examined. I think they deserve it. I'm delighted that we've had the mental strength and character to have that consistency and just keep going, being relentless. That's what we were this year, relentless. I spoke to them about how most people get to watch history happen, very few people get to actually make history. For them to do that today, for the city of Cardiff, is something that I'm very proud of."

He also reserved individual praise for Kim Bo-Kyung, who had displayed fine form in recent weeks. "I think everybody that's watched Kim this year can see that he's made to make an impression at that level. He's an international footballer and is one of the young stars of South Korea. As the season's gone on he's been more comfortable in his environment, he's learning English and he's been more adaptable. Anyone who can play in the Championship with that quality has got to have something about them and I think he's certainly one for the future."

Cardiff would be presented with the Championship trophy after their final home game, the following Saturday against **Bolton Wanderers**. One man who would miss out on the final couple of games and forthcoming celebrations was Leon

Barnett, as Norwich activated a recall clause in his loan agreement. A huge success during his eight games with the club, Mackay was keen to pay tribute to his departing centre half. "It was a tough task for Leon because he went straight into our team the day after joining us. But he played at Sheffield Wednesday in a 2–0 win and was a major influence throughout his stay with us. It's a pity Leon won't be with us when we are presented with the trophy, but we thank him for his part in what the players have achieved this season."

Having earmarked a sizeable sum to be spent on transfer activity, Vincent Tan also revealed in an interview with *The Malaysian Star* that he is keen to utilise a similar approach to South Wales rivals Swansea. "We can't afford superstar players for the time being," he explained. "We need maybe four or five new players to cover for injuries etc. We're looking. We're trying to spend smartly but it's easier said than done. I do like the Swansea model, they have shown the way. I would like to buy a Michu, who for just £2 million has performed better than Fernando Torres has for £50 million. Luck is involved on the field, but normal business rules apply off it. You buy players and they are assets. Like Michu, who cost £2 million and is worth £20 million. But if he has only one year left on his contract, you have to sell him." He also addressed the rebrand, adding: "I created some controversy with the colours. There was a lot of resistance. Most of the fans and most of the board were against it. The blogs got pretty nasty, but I would like to think I changed Cardiff's luck."

Bolton gave Cardiff a guard of honour as they took to the field, but Dougie Freedman's men were still in with a shot of making the play-offs and showed little respect to the champions once the game kicked off. Craig Bellamy returned to the side while Ben Turner and Matthew Connolly were reunited in central defence. Cardiff had the chance to take the lead in the very first minute. Kim Bo-Kyung's shot was diverted in to the path of Jordon Mutch a few yards out and his shot was brilliantly saved by Ádám Bogdán, at point-blank range. For the remainder of the half, Bolton took control, inspired by the impressive Chris Eagles. The midfielder reacted angrily to reports linking him with Cardiff in the days preceding the game, but he provided a display that will only intensify speculation. Popping up all over the pitch, he opened the scoring in the 18th minute, drilling across David Marshall after good work down the right by former Swansea full back Sam Ricketts.

Just before half-time, Eagles strode 40 yards before releasing another former Jack, Darren

Pratley, who saw his effort blocked by the legs of the Cardiff keeper. Mackay introduced Craig Noone and Tommy Smith in the second half to give his side fresh attacking impetus. He almost saw an instant return when Noone broke down the right and crossed for Smith, who was also denied by the brilliant Bogdán. Three minutes later, an Aron Gunnarsson run was halted by Craig Dawson and Noone bent the resulting free kick just inside the near post. From then on, it was all Cardiff, but they created very few clear-cut opportunities and Pratley also had the chance to punish a poor Turner back pass, but Marshall spared his defender's blushes. The game ended level both sides left the field as the stage was erected for the trophy presentation.

Each player was individually announced back on to the pitch, but the biggest cheer was reserved for Mackay, who has established a real bond with the fans and salutes them after every win with his trademark fist pump. Vincent Tan handed the trophy to team captain Mark Hudson, as the strains of 'We're Cardiff City, we'll always be blue' reverberated around the terraces. Players soaked each other with champagne and posed for photographs, managing to complete a lap of honour, as fans refrained from invading the pitch. The festivities looked set to continue for a while yet, with an open-top bus parade planned after their final game at Hull.

Sam Hammam attended the game and sat next to Tan throughout, raising hope that an agreement may be imminent for the historical Langston debt. "We are still talking and trying to find a solution," Tan revealed. "I'm sure we will find an amicable solution that is good for Cardiff City. We have some issues, but Sam Hammam attended the Bolton match as my guest and as my friend. He has a lot of knowledge of football clubs. He brought Wimbledon up from nothing to the Premier League. He can even help me and advise me on football." Now based in his native Lebanon, an honorary role has also been mooted but it remains to be seen whether a deal will see him sever his ties with the club. They did manage to settle one outstanding debt, with former Dave Jones, the problem that he claimed would eventually come to light the previous December. He lodged a High Court claim against the club for £539,000 in "outstanding bonuses" and both parties reached an amicable and confidential settlement.

Later that evening, the club hosted the annual end-of-season awards and the smart money was on either Mark Hudson or David Marshall to scoop the Player of the Year accolade. Both were signed in the summer of 2009 when their respective teams, Charlton Athletic and Norwich City, were relegated from the Championship. Despite both featuring on a regular basis ever since, they have not always been as highly regarded as both undoubtedly are at present.

Marshall was frequently criticised for his apparent discomfort at dealing with crosses and failing to command his penalty area. He lost his place to Tom Heaton on a number of occasions under Dave Jones and it was only when Mackay took charge that he was considered an automatic first choice. He has rewarded his manager's faith with a consistently high standard of performance and also appears to have all but eradicated his flaws. Mackay regards him as the best goalkeeper in the Championship and is unlikely to be in the market for a replacement in the summer.

Hudson's main weakness is his lack of pace and when he first arrived at the club, nimble attackers had a tendency to exploit this to their advantage. Like Marshall, he was poor in the 2010 play-off final defeat against Blackpool, but he has steadily improved ever since. He is a leader, rarely caught out of position or beaten in the air and puts his body on the line time and again. It transpired that Hudson claimed the top prize, with Marshall second and Andrew Taylor third. He also won Clubman of the Year and later claimed it had been "the best day of my career". Marshall did not leave empty-handed, taking home the fans' Man of the Match award, while Ben Nugent was named Young Player of the Year. More recognition followed, with confirmation that Hudson and Peter Whittingham had been named in the Championship Team of the Year, but Marshall was a surprise omission.

# A frantic finale

CARDIFF BID FAREWELL to the Championship with a thriller encounter at Hull.

4th May – Hull City (a)

Cardiff's final game of the season was largely inconsequential for them, but of extreme importance to their opponents. **Hull City** led Watford by a solitary point and needed to match their result against Leeds to secure automatic promotion and avoid the play-offs. The Bluebirds would be without joint top-scorer Heidur Helguson, who despite recovering from a calf strain was given permission to return to his family in Iceland. With his contract about to expire, the 35-year-old intended to play one final season for his local club Throttur Reykjavic before hanging up his boots. "I couldn't have wished for a better ending, than to gain promotion," Helguson revealed. "The season went great I think." Malky Mackay explained the situation by confirming:

"Heidar is going into semi-retirement to play football in Iceland and we wish him all the best. He made a huge contribution for us," he continued, praising the veteran's efforts. "With the injury to Nicky Maynard he ended up playing a lot more games than he thought he would. Heidar was the man who really stepped up to the plate. He was the battering ram for us and his overall contribution for us, not just in goals scored because he always gets eight to ten in a season, but the way he has contributed to other people scoring goals too. He's also a top pro, just the way he carries himself. He's a joy to have around the place. He's the type of character I would fill a club with. I have great admiration for him."

One of the primary reasons for sanctioning Helguson's release was the return to fitness of Nicky Maynard. After missing more than seven months of the season with a serious knee injury, he was named among the substitutes and earmarked for a brief cameo. Etien Velinkonja, an unused sub in the Bolton game, was awarded his first start of the season, after scoring prolifically for the development side. Fraizer Campbell was also on the bench and Andrew Taylor was named captain, due to the absence of Mark Hudson, Craig Bellamy and Peter Whittingham.

Amid palpable tension, the Tigers had the ball in the Cardiff net early in the game, but it was ruled out for offside. Craig Conway cut in on his right foot and saw his shot deflected narrowly wide of the far post. Stephen Quinn's pass was flicked in to the path of Robbie Brady, but his reckless effort flew high and wide. A Jordon Mutch drive was pushed away by David Stockdale, while Brady kept David Marshall busy at the other end. Cardiff fans were enjoying the occasion and did their best to wind up the home supporters by singing songs, stating that Watford were leading and going up, but the opposite was true. Due to a lengthy delay, the Watford game was 15 minutes behind and news of an opening goal for Leeds brought the biggest cheer of the day just before half-time. But before the teams returned for the second half, news of a Watford equaliser had been received.

Campbell replaced the ineffective Velikonja for the second period and was heckled by the home support for his decision to join Cardiff rather than return to Hull. Within four minutes, he had shown them exactly what they were missing. Breaking between two centre backs to receive a brilliant Kim Bo-Kyung pass, he stroked it past Stockdale to open the scoring. The contest opened up and the score was levelled nine minutes later.

Substitute Nick Proschwitz diverted Quinn's cross past Marshall to restore parity and belief. A Brady corner reached Paul McShane deep in the Cardiff area and he poked it just inside the far post after 63 minutes to give Hull the lead they desperately craved. Maynard and Rudy Gestede were introduced as Cardiff went all out to salvage the game, but their chances were dealt a blow by Taylor's dismissal in the final minute, when he received a second caution. The game looked to have slipped away when David Meyler was fouled in injury time, resulting in a Hull penalty. The award prompted a premature pitch invasion and when the fans were finally cleared, Marshall saved Proschwitz's strike. To add insult to injury, Cardiff were awarded a penalty of their own, when Abdoulaye Faye handled from an Aron Gunnarsson long throw. Up stepped Maynard, who sent Stockdale the wrong way to banish several months' worth of frustration and seal an unlikely draw. With Hull now at the mercy of Watford's efforts, there was a muted response to the final whistle and a second pitch invasion was half-hearted. But news of a late Leeds goal got the party started as Hull players returned to celebrate their dramatic promotion.

Cardiff managed to end the season with an impressive eight-game unbeaten run, which will help maintain momentum ahead of their maiden Premier League campaign. But the day belonged to a delighted Maynard, who made a goal-scoring return to the side after a frustrating season on the sidelines. "It's a massive psychological boost to play and score," he confirmed after the game. "I've been itching to do this, dying to play and hit the back of the net. Now I go into the summer with great memories of that goal. That's going to help so much over the summer before we report back for pre-season." Mackay insists that Maynard would have racked up in excess of 20 goals had he remained fit and will be hoping he can score consistently at a higher level. He will follow a strict individually-designed fitness plan over the summer and report back a week earlier than everyone else, to allow his knee to be closely monitored by the club.

The team returned to Cardiff ready for their open-top bus parade through the city. Thousands of fans turned out to see the players emerge from Cardiff Castle, replete with the Championship trophy, before boarding three buses headed for Cardiff Bay. St Mary Street was lined with well-wishers as confetti rained down on jubilant City supporters, applauding their victorious Bluebirds. They arrived at the Millennium Centre and took to the stage to address the gathered masses, clearly overwhelmed by the occasion, as the gravity of their achievements began to sink in.

"It's overwhelming. I can't take it all in," claimed Craig Bellamy. "Cardiff are in the Premier League and that's a fantastic feeling. This day is probably overdue for our club, but it's here and we are enjoying the moment. Right now it's just getting better and better. Let's make the most of it. City fans are immense. They deserve this. Players and managers come and go, but the fans are always there. The club deserves this success. We've known hard times like many clubs and now this is our moment. We've finally got there and I'll be able to sit back and watch the play-offs with absolutely no pressure."

Captain Mark Hudson added: "It's an incredible feeling. The boys deserve these celebrations. It's been a season to remember and we'll enjoy this to the full. We've achieved this together and it's right that we celebrate together."

"I've waited for this and now we're going to party," claimed loyal servant Kevin McNaughton, who would soon be celebrating the offer of a new contract. "This is our time. We are the champions and we're heading for the Premier League."

Mackay, performing his trademark fist pump and 'The Ayatollah' to the delight of fans, concluded: "It's an unbelievable turn-out, the people of Cardiff have made this a special day. They have come out to join us in celebrating promotion and the title. I thank every one of them for their support. They were with us every step of the way this season and are as much a part of what we have achieved as anybody. The players loved the bus tour, they interacted with fans along the route and it's a special day we will all remember forever. Everybody at the club deserves this day. Many of the staff have waited an awful long time. We are already planning for next season and those plans will gather pace now, but it was a time to reflect on what this group of players have done. They have put smiles on the faces of Cardiff people and we saw at close hand what it means to everybody."

The celebrations drew to a close a few days' later at the House of Lords, where Mackay, Hudson and Vincent Tan attended a reception in their honour. Former Labour leader and avid Cardiff fan Neil Kinnock provided a warm welcome, announcing: "I give unrestrained, unlimited, unqualified, unreserved, unmitigated and unbridled praise and thanks to Malky and his men." Mackay attended the League Managers' Association Awards and was named the Championship Manager of the Year, despite not winning the Manager of the Month Award during the season. The club also announced plans to take a long-term lease on land at Hensol in the Vale of Glamorgan to build their new state-of-the-art training base. Subject to council planning approval, the 40-acre site is adjacent to their current base and they hoped to commence work during the summer. The first phase of construction would incorporate five training pitches, goalkeeping, rehabilitation and development areas.

Cardiff ended the season on 87 points, eight clear of second-placed Hull and ten ahead of Watford in third. They won 15 of their 23 home games, drawing six and losing only two, while away they won ten times, again drawing six but losing on seven occasions.

The number of goals scored home and away were roughly the same, 37 and 35 respectively, but they conceded twice as many on their travels than in South Wales, 30 compared to 15, with an impressive 18 clean sheets in total. Of their 25 wins, 17 were by a solitary goal and no one player managed to reach double figures for goals scored, a first for a Championship-winning side.

Aron Gunnarsson, Heidur Helguson and Peter Whittingham all netted eight times, while Craig Noone and Craig Bellamy led the way in assists, with eight each. The success of their campaign was built on their record-breaking home form at the start of the season and three lengthy unbeaten runs – six games between November and December, nine games over the Christmas period through to February, plus an eight-game run in their final eight games. There were several standout performances; an early 3–1 win against Wolves and two comprehensive victories over Blackburn Rovers were impressive, but the 5–4 defeat at Charlton in November would appear to be the turning point in their season. Their fifth away defeat was their last until March, as Mackay revised their approach and instilled a solidarity that had previously been lacking, their "monotonous consistency".

David Marshall has maintained a very high standard of performance throughout the season. Behind a solid defence, he was never inundated with attempts on goal, but he remained focused, made key saves in pretty much every game plus stunning stops at Leeds and Watford.

With only five senior defenders to choose from, Mark Hudson, Matthew Connolly, Ben Turner, Kevin McNaughton and Andrew Taylor have all been remarkably consistent and, more importantly, adaptable. Due to absences, both short and long-term, plus the involvement of Ben Nugent, Leon Barnett and Simon

Lappin, they have played within numerous different combinations and it is a testament to those involved that disruption was kept to a minimum. Andrew Taylor, significantly improved from the previous campaign, provided a steady influence on the left, while Ben Turner remained a ferocious presence. Mark Hudson led by example while Matthew Connolly, adept at centre back or right back, proved to be a very shrewd signing, possibly the best buy of Mackay's summer spree. Kevin McNaughton was written off on several occasions, but always battled back in to contention and was rewarded with a deserved contract extension. Leon Barnett was an inspired loan signing, the right man at the right time, while the emergence of Ben Nugent was as impressive as it was unexpected and resulted in an end of season accolade. Cardiff's success was founded on defensive stability and those involved all excelled, but full backs remain a priority in the summer.

Cardiff defend as a team and the midfield proved to be a significant source of strength, in support of both defence and attack. Peter Whittingham was a huge influence in the first half of the season, netting a hat-trick against Wolves and always a threat from set-pieces. Much has been made of his lack of goals and dwindling contribution in 2013, but he has played a lot of football in the last few years and an extended break was long overdue. You would expect him to be a key man once again next season and thrive in the Premier League. Aron Gunnarsson has progressed from the fringes of the side to become indispensable. He provided a significant contribution with his hard work and important goals. Craig Conway made the most of his opportunities to become a trusted part of Mackay's plans out wide, combining creativity with a commendable work ethic. Craig Noone has been an impressive addition, a jinking winger who has contributed both goals and assists, although consistency has been an issue on occasions.

Kim Bo-Kyung was introduced gradually, but his raw talent was evident from the start. He became more influential with every passing week but his positional awareness needs work. Jordon Mutch's campaign has been hampered by injury, but he impressed in the final few months and Mackay is clearly a big fan. Expect him to have a far greater impact next season. Don Cowie was more of a peripheral figure than in his first season with the club, but he was ready, willing and able when required and scored an important goal at Sheffield Wednesday.

Tommy Smith, who filled in on both wings and

up front, offered experience and nous. He scored a significant goal at Blackpool after returning from a lengthy absence, but he never managed to recapture his fine early-season form. A wealth of midfield options has been a source of strength for Mackay, an ability to cover for injuries and poor form that he lacked during his first season in charge. But too many of those players failed to hold down a regular place and you would expect this area of the team to be reinforced in the summer as a result.

Nicky Maynard's lengthy absence was perhaps the low point of the season, but his return to the team and goal against Hull was certainly among the highlights. The signing of Etien Velinkonja has also proved to be a huge disappointment. An expensive acquisition, he has made no impact on the first team despite scoring regularly for the development side. Joe Mason failed to match the high standards set in his debut season with the club, but that was due to being used sparingly and not being able to generate any momentum. He remains one for the future. In contrast, Rudy Gestede showed signs of improvement, managed to steer clear of injury and despite a lack of starts, scored some important goals. Heidur Helguson led the line with distinction, despite his waning powers. What he lacks in pace he makes up for in experience and courage, ending the season as joint top scorer and his professional playing career as a champion.

Fraizer Campbell arrived at just the right time to breathe new life in to Cardiff's attacking endeavours. He was a goal-scoring substitute on his debut and recorded braces against Wolves and Bristol City. His Premier League experience may prove vital within an inexperienced squad.

Craig Bellamy's influence has been more subtle than some may have been expecting, but his exacting high standards were essential throughout the season. A leader of men and a local hero, he is more than just a player at Cardiff City, he is an icon and his decision to drop down a division to aid the Blues' promotion cause has cemented his legacy. His knees remain a concern, but the same concerns also apply to Maynard, Campbell and Turner, who have all endured cruciate ligament injuries. Mackay's ability to accommodate Bellamy, Campbell and Maynard may make or break their season.

Despite the impressive feats of a squad loaded with talent, nobody is under any illusion as to who is the star of the show. Malky Mackay has totally rebuilt the Cardiff side in his two seasons in charge and they are a team in his image. Honest and hard-working, with a refreshing lack of ego, he has signed his players accordingly; they have thrived under his tutelage. Where previous Cardiff sides have lacked motivation or buckled under pressure, they are now a very different beast. They have overturned deficits, scored late goals and, even in defeat, have kept plugging away and given themselves a fighting chance. They led the table from November onwards, without any serious competition, but managed to maintain their high standards and coped admirably with the pressure. He also navigated the emotive summer rebrand with class and sensitivity. Every inch the modern, up-and-coming manager, the fans adore him and he is without question Cardiff's greatest asset. He is going places, with or without Cardiff, and matching his ambition may be the club's greatest challenge. Should he remain in charge and receive the backing of the club, there is no reason why Cardiff cannot punch their weight in the Premier League. Mackay will expect nothing less.

All season tickets have already been snapped up and despite the huge sums of money on offer, a lot of work is required behind the scenes to make the club financially sustainable. There are also still plenty of disgruntled supporters who remain opposed to the rebrand despite promotion. A post-season survey by the supporters' Trust revealed that 86 per cent of their members remain against the changes. A return to blue may be unlikely, but who knows what the future may hold. Cardiff City are heading in to unchartered territory, the Blues are up. They can look forward to *Match of the Day* and going to bed a bit earlier on a Saturday night, Super Sunday, Monday night football, goal line technology and parachute payments. Finally, we are Premier League.

# Acknowledgements

I WOULD LIKE to thank the staff at Y Lolfa for making this book possible, plus Jason Perry, Leo Fortune-West and Andy Legg for their contributions. The work of Terry Phillips and Steve Tucker at Wales Online proved to be a valuable resource throughout the research and writing process, while the help of Gareth Rogers and Chris Wathan was also very much appreciated.

Finally, the creative excellence of a number of talented and generous photographers:

Jon Candy
www.flickr.com/photos/joncandy/

Andy Kearns
www.flickr.com/photos/andykearns/

Lee Smith
www.flickr.com/photos/DJLeekee/

Bartosz Nowicki
www.bartosznowicki.co.uk/

Sum of Marc
www.flickr.com/photos/sumofmarc/

Mike Vaughan
www.flickr.com/photos/mike-vaughan/

Gareth Thomas
www.flickr.com/photos/rhonddaborn/